I CLOSED
MANY EYES

A WORLD WAR II MEDIC FINALLY TALKS

BAYER NONEN ROSS
The son of Swedish immigrants who settled in Southern Minnesota, Bayer spent his military service in World War II doing his best to keep soldiers alive. His story was documented in his journal, letters he sent home, and in conversations with his family.

AUTHOR
As Told by His Brother-in-Law
Paul S. Arneson, Colonel, USAF (Retired)

Washington, DC

All rights reserved. No part of this publication may be reproduced, distributed, or transmitted in any form or by any means, including photocopying, recording, or other electronic or mechanical methods, without the prior written permission of the publisher, except in the case of brief quotations embodied in critical reviews and certain other noncommercial uses permitted by copyright law. For permission requests, write to the publisher, addressed "Attention: Permissions Coordinator," at the address below.

Paul S. Arneson, Colonel, USAF (Retired)
13300 Fort Washington Road
Fort Washington, MD 20744
www.paularneson.com

Ordering Information:
Quantity sales: Special discounts are available on quantity purchases by corporations, associations, and others. For details, contact the "Special Sales Department" at the address above. I Closed Too Many Eyes/ Paul S. Arneson, Colonel, USAF (Retired). —1st ed.

ISBN: 978-1984012784

Interior and Cover Design by Victor Rook (victorrook.com)

CONTENTS

DEDICATION .... **VI**

INTRODUCTION .... **VII**

PART ONE: BEFORE THE WAR (1917-1942) **1**

Chapter 1 The Immigrant Family: Sweden to Illinois to Colorado to Minnesota **3**

Chapter 2 Pearl Harbor Changes Everything **12**
    Waiting for the Invitation 12
    Goodbye Mountain Lake 14
    Two Weeks at the Fort Leavenworth Reception Center 15
    Eight Weeks of Combat Medic Training at Camp Barkeley Replacement Center 20
    Waiting for the Ship at Camp Kilmer New Jersey 25

PART TWO: THE WAR (1942-1945) **29**

Chapter 3 Assembling in Great Britain and Sailing to North Africa **31**
    Crossing the Atlantic 31
    Four Days at Rosneath Scotland 31
    Heading for North Africa 32

Chapter 4 North African Campaign Operation Torch **35**
    Capturing Oran 36
    Two Months in Semi-Garrison 37
    Preparing for a Move East into Tunisia 39

Chapter 5 North African Campaign Battle of Tunisia **41**
    Positioning to Meet the Germans and Italians 41
    Four Months Getting to Know Tunisia Way Too Well 42

    Next Fight: Sicily 46

Chapter 6 Invasion of Sicily Operation Husky 47
    The Initial Landing 47
    Wrapping Up in Sicily: Now What? 51

Chapter 7 Back in England Preparations for D-Day 56
    Seven Months Seems Like Forever 56
    Less Than a Month Before the Assault 63

Chapter 8 European Campaign Operation Overlord 66
    France and Belgium 67
    Finally in Germany 74
    Battle of the Bulge 80
    Crossing the Rhine 81
    The Worst Sight of All: Czechoslovakia 82
    Waiting to Go Home 84

PART THREE: AFTER THE WAR (1945-1990) 89

Chapter 9 1945-1975 91

Chapter 10 1976-1990 104

PART FOUR: FAMILY SCRAPBOOK 109

DEDICATION

I dedicate this book to Bayer's and my late sister Lois' three boys, David, Jon, and Steven, their families, and to Bayer's brother Don and his family. Also a big "Thanks, Dear" to my wife, Betty, for her patience through the writing process.

Jon and Don were of tremendous help gathering material for the book. I could not have tackled this without them. "Thank you very much"… or in Swedish…. "Tack så mycket".

Bayer and Don Ross
May 1941

INTRODUCTION

Forty-seven. That was the number stuck in my brother-in-law Bayer Ross' memory—forty-seven soldiers he had personally declared "killed in action" as a medic on the battlefield during World War II in Northern Africa, Sicily, and Europe. He was certain many more had died after he had routed them to his Regimental Aid Station but he had no way of knowing the number. His original plan was to keep track of the names of the men he had to declare KIA, but it simply wasn't possible with all the chaos screaming at him from every direction.

I've written this book for two reasons. Bayer passed away from a heart attack at the age of 72 in 1990 and many of his grandchildren never had a chance to know him. I hope I'm offering them a way to see what a truly special man he was. Secondly, I trust the book will provide incentive for others to write about someone in their family who deserves to be remembered. I can honestly say there have been very few things in life I have found more rewarding than putting this book together.

June 18, 1950 Lois and Bayer's Wedding

I certainly didn't have a book in mind back in 1950 when I was the four year old ring-bearer at my sister's wedding (yes, that's me in shorts above). Lois was 18 years older than me. My fascination with Bayer's wartime experiences started a few years later. I remember people asking him about "The War" and how quickly the conversations seemed to end. They wanted to know what he'd gone through, but he seemed determined not to discuss it. But once my own military career began in 1968, Bayer must have sensed my genuine interest in his story and slowly began opening up to me. Over many years he provided me with details about World War II that to this day I've never heard or read about from anyone else. In addition, Bayer's family had saved every letter (V-Mail) he had sent home during the war—and he wrote often. Thanks to his son Jon and his brother Donald, I've had access to those letters and to virtually hundreds of journal entries, notes, newspaper articles, war relics, and other ephemera Bayer had kept. I'll never forget the reason he gave me for his early reluctance to discuss what he went through....

> *"It's just that when I go back to that time I think about the fellows who died in my arms. God knows I closed too many eyes."*

Bayer was a combat medic attached to the:

UNIT	COMMANDER WHILE SERVING
Third Battalion	Lieutenant Colonel Charles T. Homer, Jr
16th Infantry Regiment	Colonels Henry Cheadle and later D'Alary Fechet, George Taylor, and Frederick Gibb
1st Infantry Division	Three different Major Generals
V Corps	Four different Major Generals
1st US Army	Three Lieutenant Generals commanding including General Omar Bradley
Medical Detachment of 16th Infantry Regiment	Major Charles Tegtmeyer (Regimental Surgeon after invasion of Sicily)

1st Infantry Division
Typical Organization
1944-45

- 16th Infantry Regiment
- 18th Infantry Regiment
- 26th Infantry Regiment
- HHB Division Artillery
    5th Field Artillery Regiment [155-mm]
    7th Field Artillery Regiment [105-mm]
    32nd Field Artillery Regiment [105-mm]
    33rd Field Artillery Regiment [105mm]
- 1st Reconnaissance Troop, Mechanized
- 745th Tank Battalion (attached 6 Jun 44-8 May 45)
- 634th Tank Destroyer Battalion
    (attached 1 Aug 44-6 May 45)
- 635th Tank Destroyer Battalion
    (attached 7 Jun 44-30 Sep 44)
- 703rd Tank Destroyer Battalion
    (attached 18 Dec 44-31 Dec 44)
- 103rd AAA Automatic Weapons Battalion
    (attached 16 Jun 44 -7 Feb 45, 24 Feb 45-8 May 45)
- 1st Engineer Combat Battalion
- 1st Medical Battalion
- 1st Counter-Intelligence Corps Detachment
- Headquarters Special Troops
- Headquarters Company
- Military Police Platoon
- 701st Ordnance Light Maintenance Company
- 1st Quartermaster Company
- 1st Signal Company

From 1942 to 1945 Bayer moved across Northern Africa and Sicily, landed on Omaha Beach on D-Day, and finally trekked across France, Belgium, Germany, and Czechoslovakia. Here is the chronology of events Bayer recorded in his journal:

5 July 1942 reported to Fort Leavenworth, Kansas Reception Center.
20 July 1942 reported for training at the Medical Replacement Training Center at Camp Barkeley, Texas
17 September 1942 reported for overseas deployment at Camp Kilmer, New Jersey
5 October 1942 departed port of Bayonne, NJ by ship for Liverpool England
12 October 1942 left Liverpool for Rosneath, Scotland on Grenoch (Greenock) Harbor
15 October 1942 boarded the HMS Warwick Castle
17 October 1942 left Grenoch Harbor enroute to North Africa

THE NORTH AFRICAN CAMPAIGN (OPERATION TORCH and the BATTLE OF TUNISIA)
8 November 1942 landed at Arzew Beach, Algeria
27 January 1943 at Ousseltia Valley, Tunisia
19 February 1943 at Kasserine Pass, Tunisia
5 May 1943 at Mateur, Tunisia
18 May 1943 at Oran, Algeria

INVASION OF SICILY (OPERATION HUSKY)
12 June 1943 left Oran Harbor on USS Thurston
15 June 1943 arrived in Algiers
28 June 1943 left Algiers via landing craft
13 July 1943 at Mazzarino, Sicily
21 August 1943 near Di Palma, Sicily
21 October 1943 set sail from Augusta, Sicily on HMS Maloja with stop at Algiers
5 November 1943 docked at Liverpool, England

PREPARATIONS FOR D-DAY
6 November 1944 at Litten Cheney, England

9 February 1944 at US Assault Training Center at Braunton Camp, Devon, England
17 May 1944 at marshalling area near Martinstown, Dorset, England
26 May 1944 briefed on D-Day invasion plans
1 June 1944 moved to Weymouth, England and embarked on HMS Anvil
5 June 1944 moved out of Weymouth Harbor heading for the Normandy Coast.

THE EUROPEAN CAMPAIGN (OPERATION OVERLORD)
6 June 1944 D-DAY (0445 hrs.) disembarked HMS Anvil into LCM (Landing Craft Mechanized) and landed near Colleville-Sur-Mer, France
17 June 1944 in vicinity of Cormolain, France
13 July 1944 moved to a rest area near Colombières, France
27 July 1944 moved to Marigny, France
30 July 1944 left Coutance and entered vicinity of St. Denis De Gast, France
6 August 1944 entered Mayenne, France
12-30 August 1944 moved through La Fert Macé and St. Pierre Aigle, France
3 September 1944 Regiment takes Mons, Belgium
11 September 1944 at Holset, Belgium prepared to assault the Siegfried Line and enter Germany
10 November 1944 moved from Brand to assembly area near Vicht, Germany
27 November - 5 December 1944 remained near Heistern, Germany
12 December 1944 went into Army Reserve at Dison, Belgium
18 December 1944 - 16 January 1945 around Sourbrodt, Belgium - heavy action
6 February 1945 near Gey, Germany
8-24 February 1945 preparing for assault crossing the Roer River
25 February 1945 crossed Roer and moved toward Bonn, Germany
10 March 1945 positioned near Bornheim, Germany

17 March 1945 crossed the Rhine River and positioned near Bad Honnef, Germany
18 March - 6 April 1945 in vicinity of Buren, Germany
19 April 1945 in defensive positions in Rubeland, Germany
27 April 1945 positioned in Selb, Germany on Czechoslovakian border
5 May 1945 moved across Czech border
7-8 May 1945 at Falkenau Concentration Camp Czechoslovakia.
8 June 1945 waiting in Hammelburg, Germany for orders to go home
1 October 1945 back in Mountain Lake, Minnesota

Mr. and Mrs. John Ross and Family

Front row, left to right:

John Ross (originally "Jonsson" then "Johnson" then "Ross") John emigrated from Malmo, Sweden in 1902. He had seven siblings. Mountain Lake, Minnesota's dry cleaner and tailor from 1927 until 1964.

Judith Marguerite Ross
>John and Lilly's third child. Judy married a local Mountain Lake farmer, Edwin Leslie College. They raised six children.

Lillie (also often spelled "Lilly") **Charlotte Ross** (nee Jonasson)
>Lillie had nine siblings and most became US citizens. She immigrated from Hudiksvall, Sweden in 1913 and went to Genoa, Colorado to stay with her sister, Hannah, who was married to John Ross's brother, Andrew. She married John in 1915 and they moved to Windom, Minnesota the same year.

Back Row, left to right:

Arthur Mark Ross
>John and Lilly's first child. Decided the family dry cleaning and tailoring business was not for him and moved to Chicago shortly after serving in WWII. His first wartime assignment was at Fort Brady, Michigan. From there he was assigned as an administrative aide at the Supreme Headquarters, Allied Expeditionary Force in London.

Donald John Ross
>Served in the Navy during WWII. Worked in the family dry cleaning and tailoring business for several years and then served as the Mountain Lake Postmaster. Married Lee Havemeier from New Ulm, Minnesota in 1944. Don and Lee have three children.

Bayer Nonen Ross
>Bayer reported to the Cottonwood County Courthouse in Windom, Minnesota on at 6:00 am on Sunday, July 5, 1942 and was at the Army's Fort Leavenworth Kansas Reception Center later that day. Two weeks later he was off to Camp Barkeley, Texas near Abilene for training as an Army medic. By early October he was

on a troop ship to England for the start of three years of hell in North Africa and Europe. Five years after returning from the war, Bayer married my maternal half-sister, Lois Reno. They had three sons, David, Jon, and Steven. After Bayer's father died in 1964, Bayer and Don ran the Ross Cleaners and Tailor Shop in Mountain Lake until Don became the town's Postmaster. Bayer then operated the shop until he and Lois moved to Minneapolis in 1987.

Max Orands Ross

Max served in the Army during the Korean conflict from 1951-1953 in Japan. He married Shirley Berg in 1957 and they were blessed with an adopted daughter, Jennifer. Max worked in the printing business in Minneapolis.

While this book is mostly about Bayer's wartime experiences, I also want you to know about his life in Southern Minnesota before and after the war including the story of his parent's immigration from Sweden to the United States. I believe when you've finished reading you'll see why Bayer Nonen Ross deserves to be considered a very worthy member of what Tom Brokaw has called "The Greatest Generation".

1977 Bayer in the Shop

PART ONE:
Before the War
(1917-1942)

Chapter 1

The Immigrant Family: Sweden to Illinois to Colorado to Minnesota

Before December 7, 1941 Bayer didn't really know much about his parents "story". He had turned 24 years old on November 5th but he could only remember one real conversation with his folks maybe five years earlier about how they had ended up in Mountain Lake, Minnesota after leaving Sweden in the early 1900s. That conversation hadn't really amounted to much. But Japan's bombing of Pearl Harbor changed everything. He remembered that almost overnight his folks wanted family dinners together and to stay around the table afterward to talk. The change was actually a bit unsettling. Finally a family friend confided to Bayer that his parents, John and Lillie, were petrified at the prospect of three of their boys going off to war. So for four or five months after Pearl Harbor, as they waited for the boys to be called up, Bayer's folks recounted stories night after night of their life in Sweden and the good and bad times starting out in America. The discussions did have the effect of bringing the family closer and keeping spirits up.

I'm sure you've heard of this happening before—two brothers of one family marrying two sisters of another family. In this case, here's how it happened. John Jonsson (later Ross) came from a family of eight brothers and sisters and Lillie Jonasson (note different spelling than John's) from a family of nine. In 1902, when John was only 17, he immigrated from near Malmo, Sweden with two of his brothers, Andrew and August (Gus). The three initially came to Illinois because jobs were plentiful in and around Chicago. Swedish newspapers ran advertisements for Swedes to come to work in the Illinois furniture manufacturing industry. John found his way to

Rockford, Illinois, northwest of Chicago, and landed a furniture sanding job at the Skandia Furniture Company on North Second Street. His coworkers were mainly young Swedish immigrants and although he loved having Swedish friends, he hated the monotony of hand sanding. His last job before turning in his resignation was sanding a very expensive bookcase for two weeks straight. He couldn't take it anymore. Every night he was covered with sawdust from head to toe that gave him splitting headaches.

In 1908 the three brothers decided to try their hands at homesteading together in Genoa, Colorado. Andrew was 26, John was 23, and Gus was 21. Andrew had met Hannah Jonasson, Lillie's sister, in Chicago and Hannah eventually joined the brothers in Genoa and married Andrew in 1911. She wrote her sister Lillie several letters praising the virtues of both life in Colorado and of Andrew's brother, John, as a potential husband. Hannah begged Lillie to join them. Like most settlers in eastern Colorado at that time, the brothers had decided to become crop farmers. In order for them to claim the deed for their land (three 160 acre plots each, adjacent to one another) they had to live on the property for three full years. They couldn't afford to build a house right away so they constructed a dugout with a roof of wooden planks that sufficiently covered a corner of the three parcels and lived in that for nearly four years.

By 1911 the land was now theirs but John and Gus eventually decided the pioneering life was not for them. For one thing, they quickly tired of having to shoot their way out of their dugout to avoid the constant onslaught of rattlesnakes. The two brothers decided to sell their acreage to Andrew and Hannah but before leaving Colorado John and Gus stayed to help build a house for the couple on their now 480 acre property. Once the house was habitable, Hannah made one final plea for Lillie to leave Sweden. Finally in 1913 it was "Goodbye Hudiksvall, Sweden" and "Hello Genoa, Colorado" for Lillie.

Andrew and Hannah Johnson's House Genoa, Colorado

In the spring of 1915 the brothers drove to Denver so John could officially change his last name from *Johnson* to *Ross* (it had been *Jonnson* when he left Sweden but he had kept that secret since it didn't seem "American" enough). By 1915 he had concluded that "John Johnsons" were around every corner both in Illinois and Colorado and he hated the thought of being just another one. A minister he liked in Genoa had "Ross" as his last name and John not only liked the name, but it reminded him of a place with nearly the same name near his home in Sweden. So while his brothers Andrew and Gus kept their last name "Johnson", John and Lillie were married under the new name as Mr. and Mrs. John Ross in Hugo, Colorado on June 24, 1915. Two brothers had now married two sisters!

Shortly after the wedding, the newlyweds decided to visit one of John's sisters, Maria, and her husband, John Hoffman, in Windom, Minnesota. The Hoffmans ran a dry cleaning and tailoring shop in Windom and when the Rosses visited in July 1915, Mr. Hoffman offered John Ross a job as an apprentice tailor. After a couple minutes pondering the offer, John took the job and he and Lillie decided to make Windom their new home.

The 12 years the Ross family lived in Windom (1915-1927) weren't exactly quiet ones. Four children came along in that time and in 1928 their fifth child, Max, was born in nearby Mountain Lake. During the Windom years, John Ross learned the tailoring and dry cleaning business, moved his family into four houses each progressively a bit bigger, and even tried his hand at farming again in Delft, Minnesota in 1926 with his brother Gus. Unfortunately the farming idea didn't work any better in Minnesota than it did in Colorado.

The one big event Bayer remembered occurring during those Windom years was the 135 mile family car trip to Minneapolis in August 1925 to see the President of the United States, Calvin Coolidge. Bayer was seven years old. The President's speech at the Minnesota State Fairgrounds was part of the Norse-American Immigration Centennial commemorating the landing of the first immigration ship from Norway in 1825. The Rosses, of course, were of Swedish descent rather than Norwegian, but Bayer remembered his father and mother were insistent that their children get to see the President. For Bayer, it was the longest trip by car he had ever taken and recalled that he felt so grown-up helping his Dad and older brother Arthur change a tire driving back to Windom.

I CLOSED TOO MANY EYES

1925 Arthur Bayer Judith Donald

One of the Ross's neighbors while in their last house in Windom was the Sievert Olson family. Bayer remembered one son, John Olson, who was about seven years older than himself. John and his Dad would frequent Hoffman Cleaners when Bayer was there helping greet customers. John later became the famous television announcer known as "Johnny" Olson who worked for years with Bob Barker on the television show "The Price is Right".

After those 12 years working as a tailoring apprentice for his sister's husband and also finding that farming wasn't in his future, John Ross made a big decision—he'd move his family for a fifth time; but instead of to another house in Windom, they'd move 11 miles east to Mountain Lake, Minnesota.

John had done his homework and determined he could make a better living having a tailoring and dry cleaning business of his own. He went to the bank in Mountain Lake and borrowed $200 to cover the cost of a steam press and the lease of a small building. But he had to keep a secret from the town's people until he could afford his own dry-cleaning equipment. Instead of doing the dry-cleaning at his own shop on the corner of 3rd Avenue and 9th Street, he'd use the daily train that ran TO Windom in the morning and FROM Windom at night to have the clothes cleaned at John Hoffman's shop.

Then he'd press the clothes at his own shop when they came back from Windom and no one would be the wiser. He took out an ad in the Mountain Lake Observer newspaper and in September 1927 the Ross Tailors and Cleaners was born.

Bayer turned 10 years old in November 1927 and he took an immediate interest in his Dad's new business. His brother Arthur was a year older and very shy, so he had a hard time meeting the customers coming and going from the shop and never had his heart in it. Sister Judy was only seven when the shop opened and Donald was five. Bayer started as his Dad's real helper from the beginning and eventually he and Donald took the business over years later.

> ## MOUNTAIN LAKE
> # Dry Cleaners
> ### ANNOUNCE--
> The completion of all business arrangements and are now ready to give all the work brought to us the best of attention.
>
> I have chosen this city as an ideal location for myself and family and will give its activities my interest and support.
>
> JOHN ROSS
>
> Across the street East of the Post Office
>
> Sept 1, 1927

Initial Advertisement in the MOUNTAIN LAKE OBSERVER

By 1929 John's business had outgrown the small shop and he was able to purchase a building close by. He added a retail product to his business that was turning over a very good profit—handmade men's suits. He had three basic patterns and three colors, black, brown, and dark blue. John would take the measurements, send for the pre-cut material and finish the suits in the shop including putting in buttonholes and making alterations when the suits didn't fit quite right. In 1932 he had enough in savings to install his own carbon tetrachloride dry cleaning equipment. The twice-daily sprint to the train station to deliver and pick up clothes from Windom was over!

By 1936 the business had again grown enough to require an even larger facility. He ended up buying a large stone building across from the city park on the corner of 4th Avenue and 10th Street. The business was conducted on the first floor and the family lived on the second floor.

1938 John, Bayer, and Don Ross at the New Shop

In 1939 a new dry cleaning process was available using a new product called Stoddard Solvent, and John saw the advantages in upgrading. Unfortunately, because of safety reasons, the dry-cleaning machine could not be placed in the same building in which people lived. So before the equipment was delivered John, Arthur, Bayer, Donald, and Max (11 years old at the time) built a separate facility in the backyard of the shop.

All this time Lillie Ross kept her constantly growing, moving, and working family happy and well fed. But by 1940 she was starting to get anxious about what was happening in Europe. She and John had just felt settled in Windom when World War I broke out and now Germany seemed to be behaving very similarly to the way it did then. She had four sons, three of which were of draft age or would be in a couple years, and she was terrified they'd all be called up at once.

Arthur hadn't graduated from high school. He had quit after 10th grade. The shop was growing rapidly in the mid-1930s and he made the choice not to finish school because he believed his father needed his help. John kept the shop open Monday to Friday until 10:00 pm from 1932 to 1942. On Saturdays he stayed open until midnight. Customers who came to town at night to buy clothing at Epp's or Hiebert's clothing stores expected any needed alterations to be made the same night or at least by the next day. Rather than hiring their own tailors, the clothiers subcontracted using John's skills. It was good for business, but there was little time for rest. The good news for John was that Bayer and Don became very talented tailors.

THESE ARE days when it is especially important to conserve your clothing! When you buy a suit or dress today, you buy the best you can —in the hope that it will last the Duration, and when you take it to be cleaned, you naturally expect an expert job —a job such as only Ross Cleaners can do. We'll prolong the life of your wardrobe.

Ross Cleaners

TAILORS   **PHONE 134**   **HATTERS**

Chapter 2

Pearl Harbor Changes Everything

Waiting for the Invitation

The shop was going to be closed on Sunday, December 7th, but their last dry cleaning customer didn't mosey out until midnight Saturday and John and Bayer hadn't crawled upstairs to the apartment until after 1:00 am. The family usually slept in on Sundays until around 9:00 and were coaxed out of bed by the smell of Swedish sausage and eggs Lillie would be frying, but because she knew John and Bayer had to be exhausted, today she didn't light the stove until noon. Judy, of course, had already been up a couple hours to help and Max, Don, and Arthur were downstairs cleaning the steam presses and making sure the sewing machines, hat blocks, and cleaning machines were ready to fire up on Monday.

Everyone sat down at the table at half past 12 and the last of the sausage was cleaned off the plate by 1:00. Sunday afternoons were typically free time for everyone. One did what one wanted to do—within limits, of course. Each person had their responsibilities making sure everything in the shop was ready for Monday morning's 7:00 am opening. So John and Lillie took Max for a ride to Windom to visit the Hoffmans, Arthur went to the variety store down the street to fill the sunflower vending machine, Don went to play softball with his friends, Judy spent time listening to her new "Chattanooga Choo Choo" record, and Bayer decided to take a long needed nap on the living room couch. As he usually did, Bayer turned on the living room radio with the volume low to help him sleep. Some people needed silence to sleep but Bayer could be lulled away by H.V. Kaltenborn reciting the news or even Tex Beneke singing along with Glen Miller's band.

At around 4:00 pm Bayer was jolted awake by the sound of his mother running up the stairs screaming, "Who is home? Everyone come to the living room." While they were still in Windom John and Lillie had heard that Japan had bombed Pearl Harbor and all they wanted to do was get home, turn on the radio, and talk to their kids. Arthur and Don had to be rounded up but by 6:00 pm everyone was sitting around the Supertone radio glued to the station with almost always the clearest reception—WLW AM 700 out of Ohio. They were hoping to hear Roosevelt give some assurances that their lives wouldn't be turned upside down, but they sat frozen in the living room until near midnight when it was finally announced that the President would not be speaking to Congress until the next day.

Bayer started a handwritten journal on Monday that he kept adding to for the next four years. In just the first month he recorded that Japanese warplanes attacked the Philippines and the U.S. islands of Wake and Guam, and that Japanese troops had invaded Malaya, Thailand, Burma, and Hong Kong and seized Shanghai. For a few days after Pearl Harbor and Congress's declaration of War against Japan, Bayer, Arthur, and Donald all talked about the *possibility* that they'd be going into the Army, but then on Thursday, December 11th, Germany and Italy declared war on the United States. Now the more relevant question was *where* the brothers would be sent.

By the end of December Lillie was sleepless and perpetually close to tears, waiting for the three letters from Uncle Sam inviting her sons to the war. They had registered for the draft at the Windom Courthouse months earlier. Don had subsequently been granted a deferment but when a couple of his friends decided to enlist in January he went to the Navy recruiting office and also signed up. Art was the first to be called in April 1942 and ended up serving in the Army at Fort Brady in Michigan and later at the Supreme Headquarters Allied Expeditionary Forces Europe (SHAFE) Headquarters in England and France. Don wasn't called by the Navy until early 1943 and served as a fixed gunnery instructor with tours at several stateside locations.

Bayer watched for his draft letter to arrive every day for six months. Finally in mid-June, 1942 it came:

ORDER TO REPORT FOR INDUCTION:
TO BAYER NONEN ROSS

GREETING: *Having submitted yourself to a local board composed of your neighbors for the purpose of determining your availability for training and service in the armed forces of the United States, you are hereby notified that you have now been selected for training and service in the Army. You will, therefore, report to the local board named above at 'The Cottonwood County Minnesota Courthouse" at 6:00 AM on the 5th day of July 1942.*

On the day that letter arrived, Bayer and his Dad had a serious talk. Arthur had already deployed, Don had decided to ignore his deferment and would be called up sometime soon, and now Bayer would be leaving in a couple weeks. John wanted Bayer's advice on how he should try to run the shop alone. Bayer knew this discussion would eventually happen. Both he and John knew one person couldn't possibly handle the dry cleaning and tailoring business at the level it had grown to. Unfortunately Bayer didn't have a good answer for his Dad and the worry about this weighed on him throughout the war.

Goodbye Mountain Lake
Bayer had his duffle bag packed early on Saturday night, July 4th. There were fireworks later that night in town, but no one in the family had any interest. At 5:00 am Sunday the 5th, John, Lillie, Don, Judy, Max and Bayer squeezed into the 1938 Ford V8 and headed the 11 miles to the Court House in Windom. It was Bayer's time to say goodbye. Not a fun morning.

John and Lillie Ross in their Apartment above the Shop

The family had been practically glued to the radio since December 7th and things were looking very grim in Asia, Europe and North Africa. About 30 young soon-to-be soldiers had assembled at the courthouse looking very pale on July 5th. A stern sergeant separated them into two groups, each assigned to a bus going to an Army Reception Center – one to Fort Leavenworth, Kansas and the other just 135 miles east to Fort Snelling, Minnesota. Bayer was asleep by 8:00 am on the bus for the eight hour ride to Fort Leavenworth.

Two Weeks at the Fort Leavenworth Reception Center
The bus pulled into a restaurant in Omaha about 1:00 pm for a lunch break and on the rest of the trip to Kansas the guys were finally more talkative. Nobody really knew what was in store for them.... where they would eventually go, what they'd be doing when they got there, or if they'd ever see Minnesota again. Few of them had ever left home other than a few who had gone to the 1933 Chicago World's Fair. Bayer, Arthur, Judy, and Max had done that in a car trip with their Uncle August. Don was supposed to go too, but the day before leaving he got a black eye playing softball and had to stay home.

As the bus was nearing Fort Leavenworth about 5:00 pm it passed the Leavenworth Federal Prison where a herd of buffalo were grazing in a field just outside the perimeter fence. No one on the bus had ever seen buffalo before and Bayer recalled that the sight made him feel like he had gone back a hundred years in time. Reality hit hard about 15 minutes later when the bus let everyone off at the Fort Leavenworth Reception Center.

Before the haircut at Fort Leavenworth Reception Center

Bayer thought the Leavenworth stay would be all about turning the farm boys and city kids into soldiers, but that wasn't quite what it was. There were endless forms to fill out for insurance, bonds, and allotments, uniforms and ID tags issued, testing to see which Army specialty you'd be assigned, immunizations for smallpox and typhoid, blood testing, countless films, and lectures on almost every subject you can think of. And that was just during the first couple days. The thing he WAS expecting—marching around endlessly in drill formation, running through obstacle courses, and doing hundreds of pushups—just didn't happen. But few complaints. The big event was when they posted the results of the assignment process. Bayer had to read the notice a few times before he believed it. Medic? Really? A tailor's son from a little town in Minnesota chosen to take on that kind of responsibility? He had to admit he cried a bit standing there staring at the posted order. He had a hard time imaging himself in that role, but By God, if the Army thought he could do it, he figured he'd be the best Medic he could be! He never forgot that promise to himself.

Along with his personal copy of the assignment order, Bayer got written notification that on Monday, July 20th he'd be heading to the Camp Barkeley, Texas Medical Replacement

Training Center near Abilene. So at 6:00 am on that day he jumped on another bus with 11 other medics headed to the Lone Star State. During the all-day trip he read a pamphlet entitled "FALL-IN" that had been given to him as he was leaving Windom by a member of the American Legion. He later sent it home in a letter and the family kept it for him as a souvenir of the war. It gave some interesting "Don'ts" and Do's:

THESE ARE THE DON'TS
Do not criticize your officers because you think they know less about military affairs than you do. Remember they have spent hours, days, and months, perhaps years, in study before you came into service. Let the General Staff do the worrying, it's not your job.

Do not set yourself up as a loud-mouthed authority on any one subject. You may know all about it but the other fellow does not like to be told that such is the case.

Do not try to be tough and want to show it. There's always someone who is just a little tougher and it's embarrassing when you run into him.

Do not repeat rumors you may hear. Many of those rumors are started just for the benefit of those who are willing to repeat them. Much damage is done by repeating rumors. If you do not know something is true do not repeat it. The tales that start out with "They said..." are generally pure gossip. No one has ever found out who "They" are anyway.

Do not invent stories about yourself, your family, your sweetheart or the army. Your comrades will appreciate good stories but not the kind that are created to gather sympathy or to aggrandize yourself.

Do not, when you are invited to a civilian home for entertainment or a meal, tell of the hardships or privations you think you are suffering. They may appear to be interested but they only seem so to be polite. Your looks belie your statements and they know differently. After all they are the taxpayers who are paying the defense bill and they do not appreciate being criticized indirectly. Tell them the funny things – it will make your food taste better.

Do not threaten or actually "go over the hill" or "jump ship." A desertion charge will stick to you for the rest of your life. It will deprive you of privileges and benefits until death and then transfer itself to your dependents and loved ones. It will appear in all cases of compensation and pension claims, in proving citizenship and in so many other ways. It may even deprive you of your liberty.

Do not allow yourself to become involved with the other sex in such way as to impair your health and future. A "G.O. 45" (ask your officers about it), like a desertion charge, will stick to you for life.

THESE ARE THE DO'S
Do obey the orders of your officers, whether it be General, Corporal, or a Private in command. There is nothing personal about orders. Remember as long as you obey orders the responsibility rests on those who give the orders. If you disobey, the aftermath becomes your responsibility.

Do value the traditions of your outfit. If your company, regiment, division, or squadron has distinguished itself in some past engagement, battle, or war, it is your duty to keep the spirit alive. Remember there are those who have died to keep that tradition.

Do be careful regarding the "click" or "gang" with whom you associate. Remember the old adages about "Poor Dog Tray" or the "rotten apple." You will be classified by the company you keep.

Do salute your officers as if you really meant it. The salute is not an act of servility, it is a courteous salutation exchanged by members of the armed forces of our country. The officer returns your salute in that same spirit. The service man is the only person entitled to use it from a military standpoint. It is an honor to give the salute, an honor to return it.

Do keep your uniform and equipment clean. A carelessly dressed soldier is a poor representative of the service. There are no exceptions to that rule. A dirty rifle may not fire when it is most needed; a pack, poorly packed, is harder to carry than one carefully packed. If you are to be a soldier be a good one.

Do write home as often as you can. Those at home are interested in everything you do. They are not interested in made-up stories of supposed hardships. Make your letters truthful and they will be interesting.

Do read your Bible, prayer book, or other volume of your church. Attend church services in camp and in nearby communities. You may find, as others of us found, that there are times when no other thing is as important as your faith in the Deity. Know how to call upon him when you need Him.

Class of New Medics – Camp Barkeley – Bayer in Center, Kneeling

Eight Weeks of Combat Medic Training at Camp Barkeley Replacement Center

There were four things the training in Texas provided. Medical soldiers had to be able to (1) recognize the different types of wounds and diseases, (2) provide first aid whatever the level of hostilities, (3) properly evacuate patients regardless of terrain, and (4) protect themselves from hostile fire. The course was eight weeks long; two weeks of basic military training, four weeks of technical training, and two weeks of tactical training that covered map reading and setting up a battalion aid station. Bayer thought the training was adequate, but could have been longer. He found out that the Replacement Center training **had** been 10 weeks but the need for medics was so great they had to shorten the course. One good thing he remembered about the fast-paced training at Barkeley was that his class didn't have to sleep an extended period in the hutments provided. The ceilings were so low even the shortest guy in the class couldn't stand straight up without cracking his skull. But they all laughed it off as a cruel joke imposed on medical aid trainees needing to practice the treatment of head injuries.

AUTHOR'S SUGGESTION:
Go to www.tinyurl.com/bayerross1 to read a fascinating World War II pamphlet entitled "Army Talks – Combat Medicine."

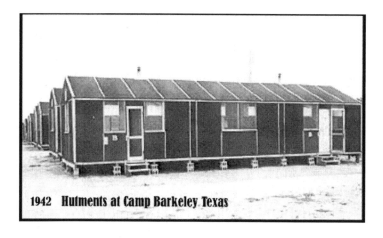

1942 Hutments at Camp Barkeley, Texas

Bayer learned the typical battlefield treatment scenario well. When a soldier is injured on the line, a voice transmission is sent back to the Battalion Aid Station, (usually 300 to 500 yards back) where litter-bearers are waiting for such calls. While they rush to the injured soldier with a litter, a unit medic administers first-aid on the spot—usually consisting of stopping the bleeding, applying sulfa powder, and bandaging. The litter team then carries the soldier to a spot where motor transport (jeep or truck) can move him to the Collecting Station which is normally a mile or two behind the line. There a physician makes a diagnosis, applies more permanent bandaging, administers blood plasma if needed, and in severe cases, injects morphine. The next transport would be to a well-staffed and equipped Clearing Station, farther in the rear where surgical procedures could be conducted if required quickly. From there the patient is taken to an Evacuation hospital still further back in the combat zone where more exhaustive treatment is available as needed. When a patient is so severely injured that return to duty is not an option, he is transported to a General Hospital outside the combat zone and perhaps returned to the States. The moves from the front line to stations further to the rear must be done as quickly as possible. The system can't afford any part to slow the movement of wounded.

The combat medics became very familiar with the packs they'd be carrying on their hips. The canvas pouch on the right hip contained surgical plasters, a hypodermic set, a hypodermic needle sterilizer, a pencil, a thermometer, safety pins, iodine swabs, carrying straps, and a book of twenty Emergency Medical Tags. The pouch on the left hip contained sterilized gauze, compressed absorbent cotton, white bandages, and a towel. They also carried sulfa powder and sulfa pills. Here is a page out of Bayer's notebook from Camp Barkeley:

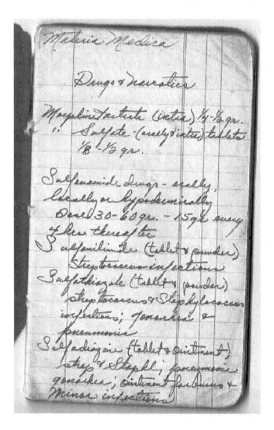

A few weeks after arriving in Texas, Bayer finally received a letter his brother Arthur had sent him in June 1942 from his post at Fort Brady, Michigan near Sault Sainte Marie. The Army had positioned thousands of troops at the Fort to protect the SOO Locks—a major shipping channel connecting Lake Superior to Lake Huron through the St. Mary's River. Ninety percent of the nation's iron ore passed through the locks on its way from the Minnesota open pit ore mines to the steel mills in Pennsylvania and Ohio. President Roosevelt was afraid that if the locks were damaged by German long-range bombers, the war effort would be seriously hampered.

Arthur's letter read:

Private Arthur Ross
Company L, 131st Infantry
Fort Brady, Michigan
June 13, 1942

Dear Bayer,
I'm not sure what your status is right now as I write this. Maybe you have already been called up but then again you might not leave Minnesota until July or August is my guess. I'm hoping for a few days of furlough soon but now what happened in Alaska by the Japs I'm not sure if I'll get it. You probably know more than me about the attack up there but I know the Jap planes hit the islands hard.
We had a parade and then a 15 mile march yesterday. They get you so tough you want to fight. I've heard that a couple boys from Minnesota have already been taken in the war. But I'm telling you that I am coming back, yes sir. At least that's what I have in my head and I hope that I'm right. But, of course, nobody really knows what will happen. Those Japs are trying to make more trouble. Oh Lord, let's get this over with quick.
I bet Mountain Lake is pretty empty now. If you get a chance to get hold of a service card put one in the shop window. It can have three stars eventually once you and Don are called up. A lot of families have four or five sons in the Army now.
Anyone's guess how long I'll be here in Michigan. There is already talk about downsizing the place. Who know where I'll go next. For sure it won't be Minnesota unless things change drastically. That's about all I think about now.

One thing for sure... the people of Sault Sainte Marie have been very good to us. Lots of invitations to dinner and some even let us date their daughters. I can tell you, we appreciate it.

Yours for Victory
Your Brother Arthur

Just before he left Texas, Bayer wrote his parents:

Camp Barkeley Texas
September 10, 1942

Dear Mother, Dad and All,
I hope you are feeling better Mother. Please slow down and also please don't worry about your boys. I heard from Arthur not long ago and he's doing just fine. He said he was likely to be shipped out of Michigan before long but not sure where he'll go next. As for me, it looks like I won't be heading to the Pacific. Not sure yet exactly where I'll go but yesterday our instructor says our class here has orders to report to Camp Kilmer in New Jersey. I have no idea how long we'll be there but probably not too long. Camp Kilmer is a place you wait for a ride overseas so I'll likely be taking a trip across the ocean soon. That will be a first for me but not the cruise I dreamed about.
We have been told that once we leave Texas our letters will likely be read by a censor and anything that gives too much detail will be cut out. So if letters I send look strange or don't make sense, it is probably because I said something I shouldn't have. We were briefed on the new V-Mail system that we'll be using. You can get the stationary at the Post Office to write to me and they photograph the letters and put them on film. I'll be able to do the same on my end. It saves a lot of weight since they don't have to transport all the mail bags.
Tell Don to write me. What has he decided to do? I hope Max is being a good helper in the shop. Make sure he does his homework since I am not there to rub his ears if he doesn't.

Your Loving Son
Bayer

Bayer's last few days at Camp Barkeley in mid-September were chaotic. He knew by then that he had been assigned to the 1st Infantry Division but that the Division had been deployed en masse to the British Isles in August on the Queen Mary from New York. The Army wanted his combat medic's class to join the Division but clearly their transport would have to be made separately. When he left for Camp Kilmer New Jersey on September 15th the Army still hadn't figured out precisely how the transport would be secured.

Waiting for the Ship at Camp Kilmer New Jersey
Kilmer was nothing like Leavenworth or Barkeley. It was more like a crowded busy city where everyone simply wore the same Army clothes. There were gyms, movie theaters, libraries, post offices, and hundreds of wooden buildings everywhere. Several train tracks fed into the camp and trains seemed to be coming and going almost constantly. Nine of the fellow medics Bayer trained with at Barkeley were also to be assigned to the 1st Infantry Division and they felt lucky to be together again at Camp Kilmer awaiting their deployment. After being there for over a week they finally got their notice that they'd be traveling together on a cargo ship to England with follow-on transportation to an undisclosed location. They were told they wouldn't know precisely where they were going until they got there. The reality or war was starting to set in.

During the more than two weeks at Kilmer, Bayer went to a camp library daily to try to get his hands on current news. He had been following the war back at home by reading the Minneapolis newspaper and while in Kansas and Texas he was basically cut off from the news and hated feeling like he was in a vacuum. Now in late September and early October 1942 he read that the British were continuing to fight with the Germans and Italians in Northern Africa over who would control the Suez Canal and have access to Middle East oil. If Britain lost control of the Canal it would be devastating for its economy and a huge boost to the economies of their enemies. In late September Hitler was boasting that Stalingrad would soon be overrun.

Every night in the barracks the ten now very close "Barkeley Buddies" would stay up late talking about the news, their friends back home, and what they figured they'd be involved with in the coming months. Bayer was especially worried now about his father's ability to run the dry cleaning business if Donald went into the Navy. He could see his parents losing the shop but also knew several ladies in Mountain Lake that could help with the tailoring if the work became too much for his Dad.

On Monday, October 5th at 6:00 am Bayer and his nine medic buddies boarded a bus that took them on an hour's trip to the Military Ocean Terminal at Bayonne, NJ where they boarded a supply ship bound for Liverpool, England. **On the day before he wrote home:**

Camp Kilmer New Jersey October 4, 1942

Dear Mother and Dad,
      Hello from New Jersey. We arrived here a couple weeks ago but only recently discovered where the Army really wanted to send us. Tomorrow I set sail to Jolly Old England but right now I doubt there are too many jolly people there. Hopefully we can bring some smiles back to their faces. I sure hope and pray for that. I haven't heard from Don for quite a while. When I talked with him last he said he and some buddies were talking about joining the Navy Air Corps. I know he was given a deferred slip because Arthur and I had already been drafted so I'm not sure why he would go in. But having said that, I totally understand in another way. We want this war over with and everyone wants to do his part. Whatever Don decides will be OK with me. Dad, I hope if Don does enlist that you won't hesitate to hire some town folks to help you in the shop. I know you might try to do everything yourself but I can tell you that would not be good. I am sure there are many wives in Mountain Lake whose husbands are gone who would be thankful for the work. At least think about that please.

I CLOSED TOO MANY EYES

Well, I need to mail this and get my stuff packed for tomorrow. Don't worry about me. The Army has trained me well.

Your Loving Son
Bayer

PART TWO:
The War
(1942-1945)

Chapter 3

Assembling in Great Britain and Sailing to North Africa

Crossing the Atlantic

There were two things Bayer especially remembered about the trip to Liverpool, England. One was the terrible smell that never left. He was used to the smell of dry cleaning fluid back at home, but this was far worse. The troops were told there was an oil leak in the engine compartment that wasn't repairable until they reached England. Nearly everyone seemed to be nauseated from the fumes. The second thing he remembered vividly was the otherwise scary serenity of the trip. Hardly anyone talked. That was not the way he expected things to be, but in retrospect he figured everyone was quiet from either being sick or scared. He admitted it – he was both.

Four Days at Rosneath Scotland

As soon as they had landed in Liverpool on October 12, Bayer's group was sent on a six hour bus ride north to Rosneath, Scotland on Greenock Harbor to meet up with his unit - the 3rd Battalion (Medical Detachment) of the 16th Infantry Regiment. The entire regiment was there waiting for something to finally happen. The unit had been in Scotland since September practicing amphibious landings but Bayer missed out on all of that. His medical training at Camp Barkeley had also been cut short, but although he felt somewhat unprepared for what was to come next, the medics who had been at Rosneath since August did the best they could to fill him in with details of what he'd missed.

AUTHOR'S SUGGESTION:
Read how the United States took control of the Scottish Base at Rosneath to prepare troops for the amphibious landings in North Africa: www.tinyurl.com/bayerross2

Heading for North Africa
On Thursday morning, October 15, 1942 the 16th Infantry Regiment boarded two ships for what everyone knew was finally time to fight...but *where* precisely they were heading, none of the troops knew. Bayer's 3rd Battalion boarded the HMS Warwick along with the Headquarters Company, Cannon Company, and the Services Company. The 1st and 2nd Battalions were on the HMS Duchess of Bedford. For a couple days the ships remained at Rosneath for continued boarding of supplies and equipment and finally on October 17th they left Greenock Harbor.

National Archives Collection   Public Domain

The Warwick stopped in Glasgow, Scotland for a few hours before heading out to sea. When they finally cleared the Scottish coast, the convoy they were part of clearly wasn't going at full power.
On Monday, November 2nd, everyone was briefed on the mission. They were heading for North Africa as part of **Operation Torch** under overall command of General Eisenhower with British Commodore Sir Andrew Browne

Cunningham assisting. The strategy was to draw German forces away from the European Eastern Front, thus relieving pressure on the Soviet Union. The ultimate objective was to secure positions to attack the German and Italian forces battling the British in Libya and Egypt. But first the pro-German Vichy French forces in Morocco and Algeria needed to be neutralized. The Americans had initially wanted to engage the Germans first on European soil, but the British thought it was foolhardy to do that this early and would lead to a huge defeat. So the British plan to invade North Africa and engage the French, Italians, and Germans had won out. The British Army had already been in Egypt to insure the Suez Canal didn't get in enemy hands and thus stop the British from using that convenient route to India. Eisenhower also wanted control of North Africa to enable the Allies to use it as a platform to eventually hit Italy and Yugoslavia

Three separate task forces would be participating In Operation Torch. Bayer's 1st Infantry Division would be part of the **Center Task Force** and was to land at Arzew, Algeria and then move a short distance west to occupy the port city of Oran. Also in the Center Task Force was the 509th Parachute Infantry Regiment, and the U.S. 1st Armored Division. Major General Lloyd Fredendall was in command of the Force's nearly 19,000 soldiers.

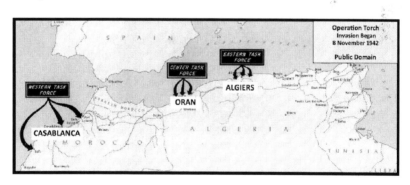

The **Western Task Force** was under the command of Major General George S. Patton and included the U.S. 2nd Armored Division and the U.S. 3rd and 9th Infantry Divisions. This force numbered over 35,000 troops and came in a 100

ship convoy directly from the U.S. Their mission was to neutralize the French naval base at Casablanca.

The **Eastern Task Force**, totaling 20,000 troops, was aimed at gaining control of the port at Algiers and was commanded by British Lieutenant-General Kenneth Anderson. It consisted of a brigade from the British 78th and the U.S. 34th Infantry Divisions, and two British commando units.

AUTHOR'S SUGGESTION:
Watch a 53-minute video on the North African Campaign: www.tinyurl.com/bayerross3

AUTHOR'S SUGGESTION:
See a condensed timeline of World War II from September 1931 – September 1945: www.tinyurl.com/bayerross4

On Friday, November 6, 1942, Bayer wrote in his journal:

My 25th birthday yesterday. Hoorah. I've never been in a place more crowded than this ship. One thing for sure—we could use more latrines. I never want to be in jail if it's anything like this. It seems like we've been at sea for a year but guess it's only been three weeks. One of the ship's crewmen told me the convoy is going far slower than they usually do. We were briefed this morning on what is happening in Europe and Africa and it isn't good but apparently the Brits are fighting a good battle right now at El Alamein in Egypt against the Germans. So now it's our turn to whip 'em. God, let's hope we do! We were told when we see the Rock of Gibraltar the landing will be soon afterward. The other thing is that the Vichy French soldiers might surrender to us at some point and if we see a white flag to treat them as nonbelligerands (sp). The French are all we should be fighting for the first few weeks. Hopefully.

Chapter 4

North African Campaign Operation Torch

On Saturday, November 7, 1942, Bayer wrote in his journal:

We were ordered to get as much rest as possible during the day today in anticipation of our landing. We passed Gibraltar awhile back so we know the war is soon to start for us. Now we're all in our gear for landing and everyone is very quiet. The Regiment commander gave a speech today saying we were among the first Americans to fight on foreign soil to help protect our allies since the First World War. Sure hope I'm around on my 26th birthday. I talked for a long time with Captain Paul Hahn who is our 3rd Battalion Medical

Detachment surgeon. He said because I am older than most of the medics he wants me to work closely with him to make sure things go as smoothly as possible. He wants to see me at least once a day to let him know if we need to move men around, if supplies are running low, and anything else I can think of. He knows I am a tailor so that should come in handy he said. Not sure I know what he means. We can't have time to do stitching when picking up men from the battlefield. He also said I should expect to be promoted fairly rapidly and to be flexible because I would probably be moved among different roles in the Regiment as things progress.

1942 Arzew Beach Landing
National Archives
Public Domain

Capturing Oran

On Sunday morning, November 8, 1942 just after midnight, the 3rd Battalion landed on the Algerian coast at Arzew Beach. For the next three days Bayer's life was sheer hell. When he got out of his landing craft and tried to wade the remaining 25 yards to the shore, a soldier's body floated up right in front of him. His first act in the war was pulling the limp body up to dry land and then dragging him behind a dune to get out of the line of fire. He knew the Army would want the soldier left there with the expectation that members of the Quartermaster's Graves Registration Unit would arrive to remove him. Bayer *did* leave him, but never forgot how difficult that was. He'd only been on African soil a half hour and had closed his first pair of eyes. He later found out that the dead soldier's body had actually been picked up by the Regimental chaplain with help from a couple infantrymen.

For the rest of Sunday, all of Monday, and up until almost noon on Tuesday, November 10th, the 3rd Battalion was on the move west toward Oran. Bayer was initially assigned to stay close behind the front and provide first aid as head of a company aid group. The litter bearers he used to transport the wounded to the collecting station soon reported that things at the station were backing up. None of the vehicles for the Battalion Medical section were offloaded from the transport ships until Oran had been secured and the fighting had stopped. For three days the seriously wounded had to be taken to the Division clearing station by anything the medics could confiscate from the locals including several horse-drawn wagons.

Two young medics from Bayer's 3rd Battalion medical section had strayed into Arzew before it had been secured and were captured by the French. Once they were identified as medics the French put them to work on their own wounded soldiers. Several hours later the medics were freed by a patrol from the 18th Infantry Regiment and were given directions to rendezvous with their own unit. Bayer said the two medics talked about that experience for days afterward. They were sure they were going to be killed when they were captured but instead being asked to treat French wounded seemed surreal. They said the French soldiers were extremely polite.

By 1:00 pm on November 10th the French in the Oran area had surrendered. The 16th Infantry Regiment had lost 24 killed in action and had 69 wounded. No one in the Regiment's Medical Unit had been killed. During a walk through the streets of Oran in the late afternoon of the 10th, the French residents clearly were happy to see the Americans and lined the streets waving and singing. The local native Algerians remained in homes for the large part.

Two Months in Semi-Garrison

For the next two months all three battalions of Bayer's regiment took semi-permanent residence near Oran occupying hotels, schools, stores, and whatever else could be found. No one had any illusions that the war in North Africa was over, but everyone had the sense that they were simply waiting for the right time to move east to engage the Italians and Germans.

On Monday, November 30, 1942, Bayer wrote in his journal:

Got terrible news today. We found out that a German U-boat sank the Warwick Castle a week or so ago as it was sailing back to England. I don't know if everyone was lost but I know there were hundreds of crewmembers on board when she left us at Arzew. I was on that ship for a long time and got to know a couple of the British fellows who worked on her very well. Those poor guys had to work in terrible conditions and under unbelievable pressure. God I hope it wasn't a total loss for those men. I'm learning that you just can't think about things too much now. If you dwell on everything every day I know eventually you'll crack. There just has to be a reason for all this mess but I'll be damned if I know what that is. So for the next week we all plan to reorganize and discuss lessons learned since we hit Africa. I know for one thing that if the medical section doesn't get equipment on time we're going to be in sorry shape. I don't like to think that we lost a few guys because we didn't have the right transportation, but it wasn't good. On a positive note, we haven't lost any medics in the Division that I know of. I was able to take a side trip today to a place where the French Foreign Legion had its beginnings called Sidi Bel Abbas. I drove our jeep and Ed Schneider and Clarence Hagel went along. We picked up a local Algerian who needed a ride. He held a chicken in a cage the whole trip. One very skinny chicken.

AUTHOR'S SUGGESTION:
See a paper describing the sinking of the Warwick Castle: www.tinyurl.com/bayerross5

On Wednesday, December 23, Bayer wrote to his parents:

December 23, 1942
Somewhere not in America

Dear Mother and Dad,
You probably won't get this letter until after Christmas but know I am thinking of you every day and hope all is well at the shop. I know you must be overwhelmed since this is your busiest time for year and I feel guilty for not being there to help. I'm certain Art and Don feel the same way. How is Judy and her family doing? I wonder if Ed's Dad took any of his hogs to the state fair this year. Mountain Lake has been pretty lucky with the College Family livestock the past few years at the fair. As you can tell, I'm thinking of you and home every day. Where I am is as different as can be from southern Minnesota. But I'm doing well – just hate to see some of the things going on over here. I couldn't have read a book that would have prepared me for this. When they say there is a whole different world "out there" they must have been thinking of where I am right now. Please tell Max to help in the shop even more than he is or I'll rub his ears good when I get home. Merry, Merry Christmas.

                                          Your Loving Son Bayer

Preparing for a Move East into Tunisia

In mid-November, the British 8th Army under British General Bernard Montgomery moved into Tunisia from Libya and British Lt. General Kenneth Anderson entered Tunisia from Algeria. By early January 1943 both the U.S. 18th and the 26th Infantry Regiments (other arms of the 1st Infantry Division) were also in Tunisia and Bayer knew that his 16th Regiment would soon follow. Finally on Sunday, January 17, 1943 Bayer's 3rd Battalion started out from near Oran and arrived about 40 miles from the Tunisian border east of Constantine, Algeria on the following Saturday afternoon.

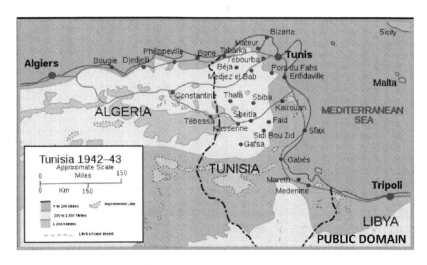

Chapter 5

North African Campaign
Battle of Tunisia

Positioning to Meet the Germans and Italians

Bayer appreciated the fact that his Battalion Surgeon, Captain Hahn, kept his team well briefed on what was likely to take place day to day. Hahn attended regular intelligence briefings and he always shared what he'd learned. Hahn now explained that American and other Allied Forces had wanted to occupy Tunisia quickly to keep it out of the hands of the Germans and Italians who were a very short distance away in Sicily. Unfortunately, the Axis Forces had moved out of Sicily faster than predicted and had become well established in and around Tunis and Bizerte. Now in mid-January 1943 the enemy in Tunisia numbered nearly 300,000 and they had brought in close to one million tons of supplies and equipment. The 1st Infantry Division was in for a fight. The Regimental Surgeon called a get-together with everyone in the medical team on Sunday, January 24th to review how he wanted the treatment and evacuation of casualties to go moving forward. He took Bayer aside after the briefing and told him he was impressed with his work and wanted him to expect being promoted early so he could act as a supervisor and trainer for younger medics. Bayer never forgot that show of confidence and made this entry in his journal the same day:

Sunday, January 24, 1943

Just finished one week of travel through the most desolate countryside I've ever seen. Northern Africa has its beautiful spots but so far to my eye they are few and far between. We have traveled for a week and have come about 450 miles. Constantine truly was beautiful – seemed almost to be a city in a gigantic hole. We moved on from there and are now near Guelma, Algeria surrounded by mountains. We're expecting orders to advance across the Tunisian border soon and when we do the sightseeing will be over and we'll be back in action I know. I hope our medical process goes better than it did when we hit Oran. At least we have the vehicles we need now to help move casualties. We need to start letting the aidmen carry plasma so we don't have to wait until the boys arrive at the aid station to inject it. I can't see why we need to wait if things aren't too rough and it can be given early. Now as we enter Tunisia we'll have to worry about malaria, typhus, cholera and dysentery. After today's briefing I was told the brass like what I've been doing so far and it was really good to hear. I think the guys who should really be thanked are the litter bearers who have one hell of a job day after day. I try to let them know how much I appreciate them as often as I can. The whole system would collapse if it weren't for these guys. I still can't believe sometimes that humans do this to themselves.... shooting at each other and then carrying them off to get patched up. I'm glad I can do what I'm doing here, but I hope someday all this won't be necessary.

Four Months Getting to Know Tunisia Way Too Well

23 February 1943 16th Infantry Regiment Troops in the Kasserine Pass Tunisia
PUBLIC DOMAIN

For Bayer's 3rd Battalion, the Tunisian campaign began on January 27, 1943 when it met up with the rest of the Regiment in the Ousseltia Valley- northeast of Kasserine- in Tunisia. In the early morning of February 19th the Regiment moved south and engaged Rommel's forces who were trying to move west to Tebessa where most U.S. troops were positioned.

AUTHOR'S SUGGESTION:
Watch a 20-minute video on the Battle of Tunisia highlighting the first engagement with the Germans at Kasserine Pass: https://tinyurl.com/bayerross6

Things were looking bleak for the Bayer and his 16th Infantry Regiment until the 20th when British reinforcements came from positions in the north and the east and eventually Rommel had to pull back from his advance on Tebessa. Near the end of March the 16th attacked Gafsa and remained there several days. The mountainous terrain throughout most of Tunisia was a nightmare for the medics. Many times line troops were asked to help assist the removal of wounded and ambulance trips to rear medical stations often took hours.

On March 29th, Bayer's 3rd Battalion Aid Station was plummeted with artillery and five of his fellow medics were killed and 8 were wounded.

The tragedy occurred during the Battle of El Guettar about 100 miles northwest of the North African German Headquarters at Gabes. The 16th Regiment was attempting to push to Gabes when it was halted by Italian forces. The battle ended on April 3rd with neither side gaining ground.

On Saturday, May 1, 1943 Bayer wrote to his brother Don:

North Africa
May 1, 1943
Dear Don,
Just a line to let you know I'm still OK. Have you had any chance to go home yet? I've been trying to locate some of the hometown boys I know are over here, but I've had no success

yet. Maybe you've heard where John Dick, Walt Dirksen, Arnold Kleimer, and Dan Neufeld ended up.

Say Don, would you do me a big favor? I'm badly in need of a cigarette lighter and a pen/pencil set. Would you please send me those articles? Not too expensive a lighter and just a cheap pen set preferably Esterbrook with an extra point. According to new postal regulations you can supposedly send packages up to five pounds overseas if you show "request by soldier". So please keep this letter. I thought it would be best if you sent these instead of Dad since you probably know more about what I want than he would. Please insure the package or I'll never get it. It's impossible to get anything over here. They certainly live differently than we do. I'll surely appreciate this Don! Dad will furnish you the money.

We were briefed on the new V-Mail service that the Army now has to get mail. There is a special piece of stationary you can get at the Post Office and they photograph your letter and I get the photo. I can do the same thing here. Let's give it a try. Sounds a bit strange but most everything does these days.

Keep 'em flying, Don!

Your Brother Bayer

By May 5th the Regiment had pushed north to Mateur, Tunisia where it stayed until the 15th when it headed back to Oran, Algeria by train to await new orders. The Axis powers had surrendered on May 13th

The 16th Infantry Regiment Medical Detachment had treated over 1,000 wounded since it had landed at Oran on November 8th. Twelve of its medics had been killed and 35 were wounded.

On Friday, May 28, 1943, Bayer wrote in his journal:

Here we are back in Oran - the same place I left in January. What I've seen since then has been rough. Yesterday we practiced landing on beaches again and I guess that means we'll be doing more of that soon for real. But where? No one seems to know. We lost far too many boys in Tunisia. The worst few days of my life so far had to be at the end of March at El

Guettar. I missed being hit by about 2 feet when a shell hit our station. I worked on two of my buddies but couldn't do any good. The Captain was completely a nervous wreck with all the work. We had to call for nearly 100 litter bearers from the Corps, and medics from the 1st and 2nd Battalions to help us. I really didn't know if we'd ever get out of there but here I am. My big hope when we go at it again somewhere is that we can get replacements for medics that are taken out of action. I haven't seen any new faces since we arrived in November and it's been just about six months. It's crazy. Yes, we had to train regular soldiers to help us just to get by – but that is not the perfect answer. Blood was another real problem. We need plasma in the hands of the line medics and I've told that to every medical officer I've seen. They agree and I know whole blood is now being stored in banks in the rear areas supplied by troops. I gave some twice. Plasma in the clearing stations and hospitals is not anywhere as good as whole blood.

Bayer gets a one-day pass to tour Algiers:

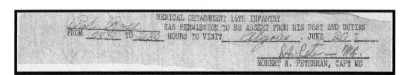

On Saturday, June 26, 1943, Bayer wrote in his journal:

A couple weeks ago we left Oran by two US Naval ships. Our battalion went aboard the USS Thurston and landed in the Algiers Harbor. Then we went by road to an area not far from Algiers called Staoueli and set up hundreds of tents and we've been here ever since. Tomorrow our Battalion has orders to report back to Algiers to load onto landing craft to go God knows where. Of the three battalions in the Regiment, the 3rd is the only one leaving tomorrow. Ain't we lucky!

USS THURSTON   National Archives   Public Domain

Next Fight: Sicily

On Wednesday, July 7, 1943, Bayer wrote in his journal:

Well, we didn't go far when we left Algiers. We went as far as Tunis and now we've been here about a week. The conditions here couldn't be much worse. It's been over 110-degrees every day, the chow is terrible and cold, and the drinking water tastes like it's been contaminated. There are a lot of sick fellows right now. This evening we were briefed that we'd be back in the landing craft tomorrow and meet up with the 1st and 2nd Battalions who are already in the Med. We'll then be assaulting the Sicilian coast southeast of a town called Gela. Our reason for this next assault: The Allies need to drive the Axis air and naval forces from the island; the Mediterranean's sea lanes must remain open, and Il Duce Mussolini has to go.

Chapter 6

Invasion of Sicily
Operation Husky

The Initial Landing

The assault on the beach near Gela was nothing like the one at Arzew. The 3rd Batallion had been tossed around so much in the landing craft that 25 years later Bayer remembered it clearly.

AUTHOR'S SUGGESTION:
Watch a 45-minute documentary on Operation Husky: www.tinyurl.com/bayerross7

At seemed like at least a third of the troops were badly seasick when they disembarked around 1:00 am on July 10th. As he recalled, there wasn't much enthusiasm among the men for going into Sicily – most had seen enough of war in Africa and now all they wanted was to go home. But once they hit the beach all that was put aside; there was a job to do and Bayer remembered it was done very well.

Once the 1st Infantry Division had secured Gela, Bayer was introduced to Captain Charles Tegtmeyer who was a medical officer in the 18th Regiment. Bayer's then boss was Captain Paul Hahn who made the introduction. Captain Tegtmeyer was soon to be promoted to Major and had advance news that he was to be made the Regimental Surgeon for Bayer's 16th Infantry Regiment. Tegtmeyer said that he was very impressed with Bayer's performance and should not be surprised if he was promoted quickly as a Medical Technician. Bayer saw this come true. He was a Private First Class when he and Tegtmeyer met and he then rose through three ranks to Technician Third Class (T/3 Staff Sergeant equivalent) in less than two years. Bayer would remain in the 16th Regiment for the remainder of the war, often called to work directly for Tegtmeyer when a medic was needed at Regiment level who was both good at training replacements and steady under pressure.

Bayer got to shake General George Patton's hand after the 16th Infantry Regiment had secured the area around the town of Troina in north central Sicily. Patton gave a speech to the 16th Regiment shortly thereafter. Troina was surrounded by mountains and the Germans and Italians had been well hidden in deep trenches when Bayer's unit advanced. There was intense artillery and mortar fire from the German 15th Panzer Grenadier Divisision lasting from July 31st until August 5th. On Tuesday, August 3rd, Bayer remembered being basically the only medic from his company not injured or sick as his unit was hit by unrelenting machine gun fire. In his journal that night he wrote that he had tended to over 35 wounded soldiers and had to declare six killed in action and that it *"...was the worst day of my life."*

CITATION FOR OAK LEAF CLUSTER TO BRONZE STAR MEDAL

Bayer N. Ross, 37451344, Technician Grade 3 (then Private First Class), Medical Detachment, 16th Infantry. For heroic achievement in connection with military operations against the enemy in the vicinity of Troina, Sicily, 3 August 1943. Repeatedly exposing himself to heavy enemy fire, Sergeant Ross fearlessly drove over hazardous roads and skillfully rendered first aid and assisted in evacuation of numerous casualties to rear positions. Sergeant Ross' heroic actions and unswerving devotion to duty exemplify the finest traditions of the Service. Residence at enlistment: Mountain Lake, Minnesota.

On August 7th the Regiment was told they had been placed in reserves for the rest of the Sicilian operation. General Patton had said it was time for them to catch their breath. For over a month they had been fighting practically non-stop. The Regiment's medical detachment had lost 16 medics and had treated over 425 injured soldiers. The U.S., British, and Canadian militaries had a total loss of over 7,000 troops.

Letter From Sicily:

Mr. and Mrs. John Ross have received a couple of letters from their son PFC BAYER N. ROSS who is with the U. S. Army in Sicily. In one of them he sent several pieces of French money. Bayer says that the franc is now worth about two cents. These pieces of money are nice souvenirs. Here is a recent letter from Bayer:

I am on the island of Sicily now as you have no doubt suspected. There was plenty of excitement on landing, but I can't go into details. By the time you receive this letter I believe the fighting will all be over on this piece of land.

I was surely glad to leave the continent of Africa, but this place did not come up to my expectations. The climate and weather compare favorably with North Africa, although I believe it is slightly cooler, but hardly worth mentioning.

Sixty per cent of the populace live within a six-mile strip of land bordering the sea. The towns are the shabbiest I've ever seen, all buildings are of concrete structure many years old. Sanitation is very poor, about the same as in North Africa, is not a little worse.

Sorry I can't tell you a little more about this place but as I've told you before, we've still got censors with us. I might mention, though, that I'm a jeep and truck driver at the present time so you see my feet are in pretty good shape. Our mail has been held up for quite some time due to this move we've made, but it will no doubt come in soon. I haven't done much writing in the past month so I'll be kept busy for a while trying to catch up.

By the way how are the fish biting back there? I'm surely sweating out the day that I can try my luck at it again.

Well, here's hoping you're all well and happy and please write soon.

BAYER

Mountain Lake Minnesota OBSERVER
September 9, 1943

Another article in the **Mountain Lake Observer** newspaper:

THURSDAY, SEPTEMBER 16, 1943

News About the Men At Various Camps

Well, we're out of pictures again. This week's showing is the last one we have a cut for. So, for the sake of this column, bring us in some more pictures of your servicemen. Help! Help!

• • •

STAFF SGT. JOHN J. DICKMAN arrived here Wednesday evening of last week, home on a 15-day furlough after participating in maneuvers that took his outfit all over the state of Tennessee. SGT. C. A. SIMPSON got here Thursday for a like furlough. John and Arny are both members of the 10th armored division. Arny is in the maintenance battalion, and John is in the medical battalion. Their home station used to be Fort Benning, Ga., but they are now based at Camp Gordon, Ga.

• • •

Also home on furlough this week is FLIGHT OFFICER GEORGE D. HESS from Lubbock, Texas, where he recently received his wings. George is now a full-fledged glider pilot. He leaves Tuesday for his new station at Bowman Field, Ky., where he will get some more training.

• • •

WILLARD FAST has been promoted to pharmacists mate third

This is PVT. BAYER ROSS, son of Mr. and Mrs. John Ross. Bayer is a veteran of both the African and Sicily campaigns and probably now is somewhere in Italy. He was inducted in August, 1942. He has two brothers in the armed forces. They are PVT. ART ROSS, now overseas, and Aviation Cadet DONALD ROSS, now taking pre-flight training in the naval air corps.

• • •

Wrapping Up in Sicily: Now What?

From early August to mid-October the 16th Regiment was semi-garrisoned about 25 miles northwest of Licata, Sicily. Bayer said that as hard as it was to believe, the men were actually getting tired of the lull in activity. A lot of time was spent exercising, playing ball, cleaning equipment, and watching a lot of movies.

On Thursday, September 30, 1943 Bayer wrote to his brother Don:

Somewhere in Sicily
September 30, 1943

Dear Don,
I hope you are doing OK kid! I heard from Andrew and Hannah yesterday. I had written them concerning a certain party out there who happens to be an uncle of a friend of mine here and by coincidence they know each other very well – in fact they're neighbors! By the way Don, Max may also know him because of your pleasure tour to Colorado a few years ago. Well anyway his name is Jacob (Jake) Ristesund. Let me know, will you?
 We still have movies several nights a week and occasionally the Red Cross puts on a show. Last week Anne Nagle (actress) and **Larry Adler** *(the harmonica whiz) were here. Jack Benny was supposed to be here too but he was sick.*
 I heard our Chicago Cubs lost the pennant to St. Louis. It would have been fun to have been at the game but I was otherwise occupied. One of these years you and I will have to get to a Cubs game. Maybe they'll win the day we're there.
 I'm sorry I can't say I'm writing this with the new pen you likely sent me but it hasn't arrived yet. My hopes are still high. One of the boys had an extra pen so I bought it for a buck.
 Keep 'em Flying, Don!
Your Brother Bayer

AUTHOR'S SUGGESTION:
See Larry Adler play his harmonica in a movie clip from the 1940s: www.tinyurl.com/bayerross8 (by the way, the lady he's playing for is June Allyson).

By mid-October it was pretty obvious the Regiment was going to be moving out of Sicily. Most thought it would be advancing into Italy but enough fellows thought they were destined to return to the States to make everyone more than a bit anxious to get the "real lowdown". Finally on Wednesday,

October 20th the Regiment packed everything up and drove to Augusta Harbor where on the 22nd they boarded the British ship HMS Maloja and set sail. Five days later they were back in the Algiers Harbor, but only to pick up supplies and a few new civilian passengers who said they were coming aboard bound for England. Their announcement was the way the Regimental troops found out their Mediterranean nightmare was over. They left Algiers October 27th.

Every day while at sea the medics attended lectures on medical supply, fractures, surgery, hygiene, venereal disease, and other topics the new Regimental Surgeon, Major (formerly Captain) Tegtmeyer, thought was important. Bayer remembers the Major asking him to stand one morning and announce that because of his tailoring skills, he would be willing to sew new rank on uniforms when soldiers were promoted. Bayer received rousing applause! Unfortunately, the Major hadn't realized how many fellows would be calling on Bayer for his sewing services over the next several days, so the offer had to be rescinded. Instead Bayer was asked to help administer sick call aboard ship and that proved to be a huge undertaking too. Over 100 people showed up in the sick bay every day with respiratory infections, coughs, colds, and dysentery. Toward the end of the trip a number of cases of malaria and jaundice were seen.

On Monday, November 1, 1943 Bayer wrote to his parents:

Somewhere On the Atlantic Ocean
November 1, 1943

Dear Mother and Dad,
Just a short note to let you know I am fine and to apologize for not writing in a while. I don't think I'll be able to mail this to you for a few days but since I have some free time I wanted to say hello. If my memory serves me correctly I was on a boat writing you last year around my birthday too. It has become a habit I guess. In years to come I plan never to be on a boat on my birthday. Dry and peaceful land is what I look forward to for the rest of my life. I suppose once again you are working like crazy at the shop, Dad. I hope you can tell me you've hired some extra help at least for the run up to Christmas. I know you don't want to take Max away from studying to help you out so tell him I want to hear that his grades are good. I have to tell you I met a boy from Windom a couple weeks ago. He often went into John Hoffman's shop there and had been in our place too once or twice. Darn if I can remember his name right

now but I'll mention it in my next letter if it comes to me. I thought that was pretty rare finding someone halfway around the world who had been in our shop. I must tell you that I have been practicing my tailoring skills lately. The boss found out I could sew so he volunteered me to put the rank on uniforms for the boys. Actually I kind of enjoy it and it helps me get to know a lot of fellows better than I might have otherwise. Well, I will write soon again. Promise! Take good care of each other.

Your Loving Son Bayer

In the same month Bayer was writing that letter to his parents, Stalin, Roosevelt, and Churchill met at the Russian Embassy in Tehran to settle a few issues including a commitment to a second front against Germany.

1943 Tehran   Stalin, Roosevelt, Churchill   National Archives/Public Domain

AUTHOR'S SUGGESTION:
See a 5-minute video on the 1943 Tehran conference:
www.tinyurl.com/bayerross10

Chapter 7

Back in England
Preparations for D-Day

On Thursday, November 4, 1943, Bayer wrote in his journal:

We've been at sea again another eight days but tomorrow they say we'll be back on dry land in Jolly 'Ol England. It just happens to be my 26th birthday tomorrow but I don't expect much of a party. Guess being in the presence of my beach assault landing party will have to do. Seems like most of the boys are pretty weary at this point. Many of them thought when we left Sicily they'd be seeing Christmas at home, but now that is clearly not happening. For one thing, it doesn't look like anything has really been resolved yet. The Germans and the Japs are still going crazy. At least I hope Italy will soon be put in its place. Seems like all we talk about now is what's next. I try not to stir things up by saying much, but it's pretty clear we're going to have to go after the Germans and Japs on their own soil.

Seven Months Seems Like Forever
Once the Maloja docked in Liverpool on November 5th, the 16th Regiment boarded trains bound for three garrison locations near Weymouth, England. The 1st Battalion went to Lyme Regis, the 2nd Battalion to Bridport, and Bayer's 3rd Battalion to Litton Cheney. Bayer said that everyone suspected that the 1st Division would be spearheading an invasion of the European continent sometime soon so it was no surprise that preparations were being made. Besides all the practice drills for amphibious landings, the cleaning and inspecting of equipment, and lectures on practically every possible subject, the Regimental Medical Detachment also ran a clinic for

soldiers in a local hospital to diagnose and treat ailments that had been put off during the past several months. Especially busy were the optometrists and the dentists. Hundreds of new glasses and dentures were fitted from November 1943 to April 1944.

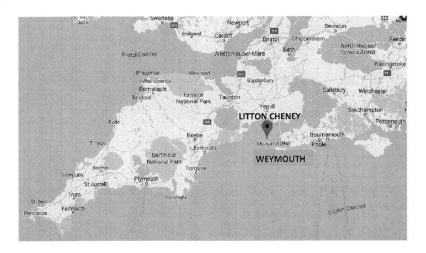

Bayer also remember that in the seven months they were living in Dorset County England many soldiers became very friendly with the local townspeople. The villagers really became supporters of the Regiment and the local pubs often treated "the 16th boys" with special favor. Just before Christmas 1943 Bayer and the other men in his Battalion Medical Detachment were invited for an evening meal at the home of a Litton Cheney physician. His wife and daughters had prepared a traditional English Christmas dinner and afterward sang songs accompanied by the doctor's wife playing a pump organ. It was the best evening Bayer said he had spent for over a year. He dated one of the daughters a few times and even thought about proposing marriage to her but decided it wasn't to be.

The fellows in the photo below are the ones Bayer was to spend the next year with.... landing with them on D-Day on Omaha Beach and trudging through France, Belgium, Germany, and Czechoslovakia.

**1944 Prior to D-Day Invasion
Dorset England
Medical Detachment to 3rd Battalion,
16th Infantry, 1st Infantry Division**
Front Left to Right: Sgt. Morton, Capt Hahn, Avagliano, Gilden, Smith, Spector
Back Left to Right: Winters, Smith, Ross, Steele, Cochran, Russo, Nunn, Spitz

I CLOSED TOO MANY EYES

A note on a couple of these men:

Captain Paul Hahn was wounded first by a shell fragment on July 11, 1943 during a tank break through. He was removed for treatment after six hours. He received a second wound on D-Day on Omaha Beach in France. Fragments from a mortar fire fractured his pelvic bone and lodged in his abdomen. He was evacuated by air on July 19, 1944 to Crile General hospital in Cleveland. He received his medical degree in 1937 from Ohio State University. Bayer was the medic who attended to him after he was wounded the second time. Although Bayer had just been wounded himself, he performed first aid on Captain Hahn and helped the litter bearers move him to the Regimental aid station.

Matthew "Matty" Avagliano was one of Bayer's closest friends during the war and one he thought had been killed and never found. It turned out Avagliano had been captured by the Germans on November 23, 1944 and sent to a prisoner-of-war camp near Neubrandenburg, Germany called Camp Fünfeichen. The camp was liberated on April 28, 1945 when a Soviet armored division reached Neubrandenburg. In 1994 the newspaper in Avagliano's hometown of Hoboken, New Jersey ran a story about him which included the photo shown below:

Everyone in the Regiment got a few specially printed Christmas cards to send to friends and family. The one below was sent to his family in Mountain Lake and they kept it tied up with all the correspondence they received from their three boys during the war.

Bayer included a note to his parents with the Christmas card:

Somewhere in England
December 24, 1943

Dear Mother and Dad,
Sure wish we could all be together today and tomorrow but looks that we may have to wait until next year to celebrate Christmas together. Surely by then things will be back to normal. Many thanks for the package you sent. I have to admit I opened it early and sure liked the cigarettes and the 127 film

and the cookies you made Mother. I had to share the cookies a bit so if you ever make more there are several boys who look forward to seconds. I'll be meeting Arthur soon when the two of us get furloughs together. We talk on the phone once in a while but it's hard to hear him for some reason. I got a card from Don and Lee and they sound fine. Also a card from Judy and Ed. I was glad to hear that the shop hasn't driven you crazy yet Dad. It was good that you were able to hire some extra help for the holidays. Maybe you can keep them on the payroll until Don and I get home. I've been promoted so now you have a sergeant for a son. I don't see much change in my life yet because of that, but the extra few dollars don't hurt.

 Three nights ago a doctor's family in the town we're in invited eight of us to their home for an early Christmas dinner. They served an appetizer I had never heard of called "Devils on Horseback". Apparently it can be made several different ways but ours were made with dates and chutney wrapped in bacon—and fried. The turkey dinner was much like we have at home and it was followed by plum pudding for dessert. After dinner we sang Christmas carols while the doctor's wife accompanied us on their organ. The townspeople here really treat us all very nice. One of their daughters, Christina, was especially nice and offered me a tour of the surrounding countryside when I am able to get a pass for a day. I told her I'd try to get one as soon as I could.

 I'll say goodbye for today and Wish You a.....

Very Merry Christmas
Your Loving Son Bayer

Litton Cheney, Dorset England

On Thursday, March 30, 1944, Bayer wrote in his journal:

I'll give the Army credit for keeping us busy and our minds off the inevitable, but everyone knows and is talking about what has to be coming soon. The Regiment has now had several practice beach landings and I doubt we're doing that for no reason. Everyone is convinced we will be the first unit to go into battle in Europe but just exactly when and where is anyone's guess. At a pub I went to the other night one of the local fellows said that it was widely felt we were stationed near the southern shore of England in case the Germans invaded. I can't believe the Germans would be that stupid. Clearly we are the ones that will be going after them or we wouldn't need all this beach landing practice. It just has to be soon. We've heard the Germans are all over the European continent and it's more than time to shut them down.

On Friday, April 28, 1944, Bayer wrote in his journal:

It has to be getting close. We were recently issued sand bags for all our vehicles. Plus a lot of our medical equipment and supplies have been waterproofed. We've been told to expect the word to soon come down to waterproof the vehicles. Tonight I was able to get in to see the movie "The Miracle of Morgan's Creek" with Betty Hutton and a fellow whose name I can't recall. Probably one of the best shows I've seen in a long time.

AUTHOR'S SUGGESTION:
See the movie trailer for "The Miracle of Morgan's Creek": www.tinyurl.com/bayerross9

Less Than a Month Before the Assault

On Wednesday, May 31, 1944, Bayer wrote in his journal:

We wait no more. We've moved twice this month, each time getting closer to the coast of England where we'll be launching from the port of Weymouth. All our equipment has been waterproofed and packaged for movement. We're now totally restricted to the camp and a few days ago we were briefed on the plan. We'll be performing an assault landing on the northern coast of France near a place called Colleville-Sur-Mer and our Regiment will lead the charge. I guess we're definitely part of history. On Sunday everyone got their own personal life preserver and a Finance Officer gave us French Francs in exchange for the money we'd turned in earlier. Not exactly sure what I'll be buying. I doubt a ticket home will be an option. I have to say that everyone seems ready to get going so we can get this all over with. The briefings we got sure made it seem like the big boys had put a lot of thought into everything. Major Tegtmeyer has asked that I help set up the Regimental Aid Station behind some Roman ruins that should be plainly visible as soon as I hit the beach. The next day we'll move it closer to town. He also told me I was soon to be promoted to Technician Grade 5 and be called Corporal- but right now that's the last thing on my mind.

AUTHOR'S SUGGESTION:

See a 20-minute video that shows how the Allies readied in England for the D-Day invasion:
www.tinyurl.com/bayerross11

Three short videos that will help you understand the preparations in Weymouth for D-Day:
www.tinyurl.com/bayerross12
www.tinyurl.com/bayerross13
www.tinyurl.com/bayerross15

Early June 1944
Weymouth England
1st Infantry Division Loading Up
Prior to Assaulting Omaha Beach
National Archives / Public Domain

Chapter 8

European Campaign
Operation Overlord

Early in the morning of Thursday, June 1, 1944 the Regiment traveled by convoy from the marshalling area to Weymouth. Bayer's 3rd Battalion went aboard the HMS Anvil. The Regimental Medical Section instead went aboard the USS Chase which confused Bayer a bit. Since the Regimental Surgeon had asked him to help set up his aid station on the beach upon landing, he figured he would be ordered to accompany Major Tegtmeyer on his troop ship - but that didn't happen. As fate would have it, Bayer couldn't have helped with the aid station anyway, as he would be wounded soon after hitting the beach and the aid station had already been set up by the time he got there needing what he said was "…just some patching up". More about that later.

Once the Battalion had settled aboard the Anvil, Bayer assumed they'd be heading straight for France. That didn't happen. He later heard that the weather was to blame. The troops had been briefed in advance that the sky needed to be clear, the moon full, the winds low, and the seas calm or a delay could happen. Finally, early in the morning of June 5, 1944 the elements must have come together because the Regiment headed out of Weymouth Harbor. D-Day was at hand.

France and Belgium
Bayer said the one day trip from England to France was the most surreal 24 hours of his life and very similar to the time spent sailing to North Africa. It was eerily quiet as almost everyone seemed to be in deep thought. There was hardly no room to move, it seemed half the fellows were seasick, the boat reeked of fumes, and everyone was pathetically uncomfortable because of the weight of everything slung on their backs. Plus everyone was starved. Before boarding the troop ship, no one had eaten for at least 8 hours and on the ship all they had was coffee and biscuits. Bayer remembered thinking this was NOT the way an army should be positioned before being expected to perform at peak performance. But there they were.

D-Day June 6, 1944
1st Infantry Division
Landing on Omaha Beach
National Archives Public Domain

At about 3:00 am on Tuesday, June 6th, the wait was over. Bayer remembers being one of the first off the Anvil and dropping down the side into an LCM (Landing Craft Mechanized) which continued bouncing like an out of control carnival ride toward shore. Men were getting sick, bouncing into each other, holding their rifles up and trying to remove the weather proofing, all in anticipation of the door opening so they could dash into hell. Bayer remembered thinking this must be the way it feels to enter the actual Hell.

It was not an easy stride to the shore once that LCM door crashed open. The sound of machine-gun bullets was continuous and all Bayer knew to do was try to ignore it and look for wounded. He remembers that the Quartermaster troops that should have been present to remove casualties weren't to be seen so Bayer once again had to recruit combat soldiers to help him. As much as possible injured soldiers were initially moved to a protective rock wall just about 25 yards from the shoreline.

June 6, 1944
Omaha Beach
Troops of 3rd Battalion, 16th Inf Regiment
National Archives   Public Domain

In the five to six hours after landing, Bayer was sure he had attended to at least 20 soldiers who had been injured and had to declare at least five or six killed in action. He thought it was around noon that *he* was hit. He had left the wall barrier to pull another soldier further inland when he heard what he thought was something exploding on his belt. He said it took a minute or two before he realized the sound was from the first aid kit on his left hip being hit. The bullet had glanced off and passed through his left hip. He managed to continue dragging the soldier on the ground to the wall barrier and then another medic looked at Bayer's wound.

The bullet had not caused any bone or organ damage and Bayer remembers continuing to work on other soldiers for a couple more hours after having had sulfa powder sprinkled on his entry and exit wounds and bandaged. Finally he felt too weak to be productive and found his way to the Regimental aid station. Major Tegtmeyer saw him and jokingly chastised him for reporting for duty at the station with a "broken wing." The Major administered blood plasma, changed the dressings, and reluctantly (after Bayer's pleading) allowed him to return to work. Bayer remembers that although the pain was rough for a couple days he always felt exceptionally lucky. Clearly, he thought, things could have been much worse! While he was attending to Bayer, Major Tegtmeyer told him that as of July 1st Bayer was to be promoted to Technician Grade 5 and that he was going to recommend him for early promotion to Technician Grade 4 (Sergeant) within a few months.

CITATION FOR BRONZE STAR MEDAL

Bayer N. Ross, 37451344, Technician Grade 4, Medical Detachment, 16th Infantry. For heroic achievement in connection with military operations against the enemy in the vicinity of Colleville-sur-Mer, Normandy, France, 6 June 1944. Disregarding heavy artillery, machine-gun, and small-arms fire, Sergeant Ross courageously remained in exposed territory to render first aid and evacuate numerous wounded comrades. His coolness and skill under fire were responsible for saving of many lives and bolstering the morale of assault elements. Residence at enlistment: Mountain Lake, Minnesota.

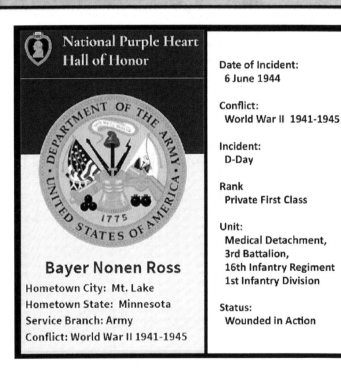

National Purple Heart Hall of Honor

Bayer Nonen Ross
Hometown City: Mt. Lake
Hometown State: Minnesota
Service Branch: Army
Conflict: World War II 1941-1945

Date of Incident:
6 June 1944

Conflict:
World War II 1941-1945

Incident:
D-Day

Rank
Private First Class

Unit:
Medical Detachment,
3rd Battalion,
16th Infantry Regiment
1st Infantry Division

Status:
Wounded in Action

By nightfall the Regimental aid station had about 75 wounded soldiers. Around 10:00 pm Bayer helped take several of them to the beach where they went aboard emptied landing craft for transport back to hospitals in England. Days later it was disclosed that on D-Day over 500 men in the 16th Infantry

Regiment had been wounded, over 350 were missing in action, and at least were 50 killed in action.

AUTHOR'S SUGGESTION:
See a riveting 47-minute video entitled "Slaughter at Omaha Beach": www.tinyurl.com/bayerross16.

Also, here are three short videos documenting the landing on Omaha by the 16th Infantry Regiment:
www.tinyurl.com/bayerross17
www.tinyurl.com/bayerross18
www.tinyurl.com/bayerross19

For the next 10 days the Regiment continued fighting its way westward until it reached Colombieres when it was ordered to hold. Until July 20th the men stood down and performed equipment repair and replacement, trained reinforcements, and caught their breath. Bayer said the time spent there really improved morale.

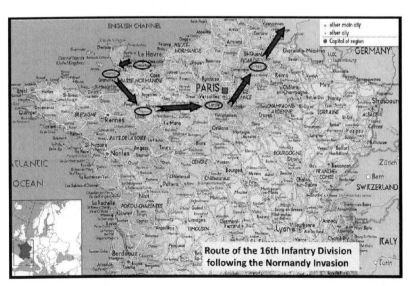
Route of the 16th Infantry Division following the Normandy Invasion

On Thursday, September 1, 1944 Bayer wrote in his journal:

Well, guess I'm not the same fellow who went in the Army about two years ago. I never thought one person could see this much horror in a lifetime! I feel like I'm 76 instead of 26. But we all have to keep our wits about us because we have the feeling if we don't win this it won't be worth living. So since we landed in France in June it has been constant movement except for a week or so early on. Since then we've advanced pretty much constantly and have been in attack mode the whole time. The worst so far was probably in late July around Coutances. One morning we had probably 1000 or more bombers hit enemy positions just ahead of us and then the Regiment went at it with all we had. We ran out of litter bearers and ambulances and had to call for help. Major Tegtmeyer came to our aid station to lend a hand. It was absolutely the worst mess I have ever seen. But thank God I'm still here to write this. I haven't had a cigarette in probably 10 days but not sure I miss them or not. I'm so wound up I doubt they would help. In early-August (seems forever but really only a few weeks ago) we had German bombers hit our assembly area and we had about a dozen casualties. Now as I write this we've just completed a 150 mile trip and are getting close to the Belgian border. We've skirted around Paris but never saw more than the city lights. I never thought if I were ever lucky enough to get <u>this close</u> to Paris I wouldn't be able to stop and see it. C'est la vie....

Two days after writing the above journal entry, the 16th Regiment took control of Mons, Belgium. In doing so they came upon a German Corp that was trying to head back to Germany but had been stopped by Allied bombing. The Regiment took hundreds of German prisoners who surrendered with the understanding that their wounded would be attended to.

On Wednesday, September 6, 1944 Bayer wrote in his journal:

I can't believe what just happened these past few days. We're in Belgium now and we've spent two days patching up German soldiers by the hundreds. I certainly don't mind because if they're in our care they're not shooting us, but it does seem odd to be doing this nonetheless. For those needing more help than we can give them at the aid station, we're sending to the civilian hospital at Mons. I guess we're not too concerned that the severely injured will be able to be much of a threat any time soon. We've been briefed that from here we continue heading to Germany but that it will be no easy task. The Germans built the Siegfried Line years ago that has been rebuilt. Almost the whole German border is protected with bunkers and tank traps. But to get this mess over with we have to penetrate it and neutralize the Jerrys on their own soil.

Finally in Germany

1944 Crossing the Siegfried Line

National Archives Public Domain

Over the next few weeks Bayer collected several propaganda leaflets that Germany literally threw at our soldiers. Here are a few he brought home:

Americans to the Front!

Have you ever thought of how this war against Germany will end? Suppose, America wins and Germany is beaten, what will happen to you? Have you ever thought of that?

A new war, the Third World War would be the subsequence: Democracies against Bolshevism. Just picture the whole Balkan in the fangs of the Russians, the Mediterranean Sea a sphere of Bolshevistic influence.

Is it American Interests that are thus jeopardized?

Certainly not – but British interests!

In that case you have to keep on fighting — fighting England's fight. You will be dragged over more battlefields, thousands of miles away from America. No leave — for how many years? Playing sucker for England. How does this idea appeal to you?

The war-mongers will not ask you whether you like or not. They will get a kick out of you — and money besides.

But You May Feel Proud – Heeding the Call

"Americans to the Front"

LISTEN, YANK:

ARE YOU A SUCKER?

No doubt you have heard the saying, credited to Old Man Barnum, that there is a sucker born every minute.

But has anyone ever dared to call you a sucker and got away with it? I guess not! At home you would have knocked hell out of anyone trying to make a sucker out of you. But that was quite some time ago, when you were still living in the good old States, when you were still free, white and over twenty-one.

You are in the Army and have to obey orders. And that is as it should be, for, in time of war, there must be soldiers and soldiers need discipline.

But what would you do, in case somebody called you a **sucker, a sucker in uniform?**

Now, don't fly up, keep your shirt on. Think it over, Yank!

Aren't you the real sucker of this war?

Winter is approaching and you fellows are literally left in the cold. Instead of living comfortably at home, tending your jobs, staying with the folks and having your fun, going out to dances, to the movies etc, they have sent you to Europe to fight a war you have no interest in whatsoever.

Well, Yank, if you ain't a sucker, what would you call a man who, for the sole benefit of a bunch of god damned jews lets himself into a mess, where he has all the chances of getting killed or maimed for life?

Come clean, Yank and don't give us for an answer that you have been foolish enough to believe that old bunk of making the world safe for Democracy. The boys fell for that in 1917/18. But do you remember what the same boys said when they returned to the USA?

AND NOW IT IS YOUR TURN TO BE FOOLED!

It is almost the same picture to-day as then, only it is **Roosevelt** instead of **Wilson** and the scape-goat this time is **Hitler** instead of the **Kaiser**. The rest is the same.

Now as then big business and the international bankers behind the scenes of the theatre of war, pulling the strings, the jews blowing the trumpets of advance, in the meantime staying wisely out of the firing-line and in the midst of it, you, the suckers, suffering, bleeding, dying in agony. There is only one striking difference between 1944 and 1918 and that difference is the Germany of then and the Germany of to-day.

We Germans are not licked yet, not by a long shot!

We will have some surprises for you before long that will make you wish you had never set your foot on European soil.

In the meantime we shall stand our ground, waiting for you boys to come over the top, feeling confidently that we can and will lick you any time and any place you fellows should choose to bust into us.

And in case you want to know what gives us that confidence, here is our answer: A man that fights in the defence of his own soil, for the protection of his family, his home and his freedom will always be superior to a force of suckers!

> Why, you Yanks are nothing but the henchmen of a couple of lousy, stinking kikes, the mercenaries of a bunch of crooked politicians.

Alright, get boiled up over this and be mad at us for saying so, for calling a spade a spade.

The fact remains and on the long run you yourself will see, that

YOU ARE THE REAL SUCKERS OF THIS WAR!

P. S. Pardon our rather strong language but we felt it necessary to give you our opinion. Take it or leave it.

Jerry

... Blondes prefer strong and healthy men

... not cripples!

You're sure you will be lucky?

That's exactly what all the tens of thousands of cripples and maimed thought before they were hit...

On Saturday, September 30, 1944 Bayer wrote in his journal:

It has happened! The old Capital of Germany...Aachen... right on the Siegfried Line is being surrounded but the Germans don't want to let go. Hitler has apparently said the old city would be defended until the last German fell, so we know what we have to do. We took one hell of a beating from the 15th until just a couple nights ago when the shelling finally stopped. For almost two weeks I bet I didn't get over 50 hours of sleep in total and never over 3-4 hours at a time. But thank God we're still pushing on although many of my buddies haven't been so lucky. Once Aachen is tied down we are supposed to be heading east. Not exactly sure where we'll go but I wouldn't be shocked if I got to see Berlin. Someone in this man's outfit had better see it. I miss letter call but I don't know how they'd get letters to us right now. Hopefully soon!

AUTHOR'S SUGGESTION:
See a 2-minute video entitled "Allies Battle for Aachen": www.tinyurl.com/bayerross20

On Saturday, November 25, 1944 Bayer wrote in his journal:

I'm just in a fog. My buddy Matty Avagliano hasn't been seen since Wednesday night. He was driving a jeep back from the Regimental aid station. We know he had arrived there about 10:00 pm but no one has seen or heard from him since. I should have gone with him but we were so busy at the Battalion I just couldn't break away. I don't know if he was wearing the arm band or not. Sure am praying he's OK. It won't be the same if I can't have him to talk to when things get bad. And things get bad a lot. I bet there aren't 20 medics in the whole regiment that were with me in Sicily. Training new guys coming in is almost an everyday thing. It's pathetic what they don't know when they arrive. Had a very odd birthday on the 5th. Bet there wasn't a birthday cake within 200 miles. Actually I felt pretty good about what we were doing on my birthday.

We took in about 100 older civilians that had fled Aachen and treated them with medications we could get from local hospitals – mostly insulin. Some of these poor old folks were close to expiring from dehydration, blood sugar shock, pneumonia, and more. We got a lot of hugs and the whole experience really left us wondering what all this mess is truly all about. Hitler and his sidekicks need to go.

I doubt most of the civilians I've met have any idea what he's doing.

Battle of the Bulge
Shortly after Bayer made that last journal entry, western Germany, Luxembourg, and Belgium exploded with Hitler's last big attempt at breaking through the Allied front and turning the war in his favor by splitting the British and American forces in two. Winston Churchill was to call the Battle of the Bulge waged mainly in the Ardennes Forest "the greatest American battle of the war." It raged on from December 16, 1944 to January 25, 1945.

There were over 80,000 American casualties (19,000 killed, 47,500 wounded, and 23,000 captured or missing). While it was an Allied victory, it did delay the plans to move eastward by several weeks.

AUTHOR'S SUGGESTION:
See a 4-minute video on the Battle of the Bulge: www.tinyurl.com/bayerross21

On Saturday March 10, 1945 Bayer wrote in his journal:

Matty Avagliano never turned up. I've witnessed just about every horror imaginable these past couple years, but Matty's disappearance has really hurt. He wanted me to visit him in New Jersey when all this is over. Guess that won't happen. So now it's March and things are fairly quiet after the worst four months so far. I have to believe this war is soon over. The Jerrys gave us just about everything they could in that God forsaken snow covered forest and we've pushed them back. I can't tell you how many deserted tanks we found as we plowed back through the Siegfried Line again and now we're sitting between Cologne and Bonn as of this week. We crossed the Roer River a couple weeks ago on the narrowest foot bridges imaginable - but it worked. Sadly a couple days ago one of our medics driving a jeep hit a mine and was killed along with two other boys. Lt. Keuchler was wounded.

I've now been promoted again. Something tells me the Army might want me to stay in after the war. (Sorry Uncle Sam). Good news to end this page – we were told late today that we have taken control of a major bridge across the Rhine at a place called Remagen. We'll be heading across the Rhine soon too.

Crossing the Rhine
From March 10-17, 1945 Bayer's Regiment stayed in Bornheim just north of Bonn, The troops had a chance to live a semi-normal life with bath tubs, clothes washing equipment, and American movies shown in confiscated German theaters. Late in the afternoon on Saturday the 17th the Regiment crossed over the Rhine by motor convoy and took a position in Bad Honnef.

1945 Crossing the Rhine Near Bonn

On Saturday, April 7, 1945 Bayer wrote in his journal:

Since we crossed the Rhine the Germans have seemed to be fighting harder than ever before. We're sure the Nazi Generals are about ready to scream and are taking it out on the troops. We're now near the Weser River maybe 100 miles northeast of Bonn and we'll soon be crossing it and pushing our way east I suppose.

On Saturday, April 28, 1945 Bayer wrote in his journal:

Selb, Czechoslovakia. We fought our way through the Harz Mountains and I do mean fought. We really thought the Jerrys would be letting up by now but we don't seem to gain much ground without a high cost. When we were in Sulzhayn we used some captured German medics as litter bearers. They seemed relieved in a way that we didn't stick them immediately in a POW camp. That might come later. We had a couple quiet days in Holdenstadt and then yesterday we convoyed over a hundred miles to get here in Selb.

The Worst Sight of All: Czechoslovakia
Bayer and I talked about his wartime experiences several times over the years but never about what he witnessed near the end of the conflict in Czechoslovakia. Finally during our last "war

chat" he started to open up about May 7th and 8th of 1945 and I could see he was in pain as he choked back tears. In taking the towns of Franzenbad and Cheb the 16th Regiment had discovered the Falkenau Concentration Camp. The Regimental Commander had asked for some medics to inspect the camp with him and Bayer volunteered not really knowing what to expect. Here are a couple photos he took:

Also in the inspection group from the Regiment was a Sergeant Samuel Fuller who after the war became a well-known Hollywood screenwriter and film director. On the inspection of the concentration camp Sam used a movie camera his mother had sent him to record what they saw. Years later the film he had informally labeled "V-E+1", became part of a French documentary "Falkenau: The Impossible (1988)." I strongly recommend you see the four parts of the French video:

(1) www.tinyurl.com/bayerross22
(2) www.tinyurl.com/bayerross23
(3) www.tinyurl.com/bayerross24
(4) www.tinyurl.com/bayerross25

Waiting to Go Home

Bayer believed the most bizarre event for him during the war occurred as the inspection group was walking out of the Falkenau camp on May 8th. Just as they were leaving the gate someone shouted "THE WAR IS OVER!" Bayer said the crying and the laughing more or less cancelled each other out at that moment and all that was left was numbness. He just wanted to go home.

But four more months had to go by before Bayer was home. During June, July, and most of August he had an office and sleeping room at 22 Kissinger Strasse, Hammelburg, Germany as part of the U.S. Occupation Force. Toward the end of August he was transferred to a tent city called Camp Twenty Grand near Le Havre, France waiting for the ship to New York. From New York it was by train to Minneapolis, and finally a bus ride to Mountain Lake on Monday, October 1, 1945.

A few words about Camp Twenty Grand. It was one of about a dozen tent cities set up around Le Havre to house troops coming to and going from the European Theater of Operations. Incoming troops would stay in one of these camps until his assignment was determined and he was sent to the exact location. For troops like Bayer waiting to go home, the camp was the place to stay until your ship arrived. The camps were all named after American brand cigarettes: Twenty Grand, Lucky Strike, Old Gold, Phillip Morris, etc.

AUTHOR'S SUGGESTION:
See a video and a website description of the "cigarette camps": www.tinyurl.com/bayerross26 www.tinyurl.com/bayerross27

While Bayer was at the camp, he got several passes to go to Paris. Here is what a pass looked like and some souvenirs he brought back:

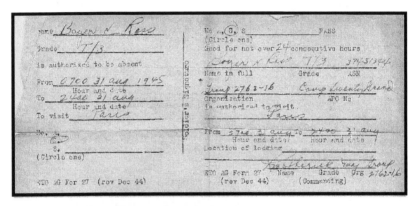

PAUL S. ARNESON

While still in Czechoslovakia, Bayer wrote the following letter to his brother Don and his new wife Lee:

Czechoslovakia
May 30, 1945

Dear Don and Lee,
Haven't much to do this afternoon so have been sitting by the window watching people walk by (especially the sweater girls) so thought I'd drop you a few lines to keep my mind occupied. I just haven't been myself lately since some of my buddies have left for home. They had more points than I do. After living with them for almost three years through thick and thin (mainly thick), I can't get over their absence in a day. I was so glad to find out that one of those who got to go home was Matty Avagliano who had been a POW for many months in a camp north of Berlin. I just found that out yesterday. Maybe one of these days I'll be lucky enough to get home myself. I've got 103 points now and I understand I'll get 10 additional points for the past two campaigns. That ought to take me home unless they get some funny ideas.

We've got movies here now and I make sure I don't miss any. Got to catch up on what I've missed you know. Some of them are so old I can remember seeing them before leaving for the Army.

Gosh, it must be nice back in Minnesota now. Surely will love to get back there. Sometimes wonder if I'll be content to stay in one place after I get home. Afraid I might get the wandering fever. This Army does things to a guy you know.

School must be over for Maxie now. Wonder how his grades were. He never would tell me. Must have been rather hard on him though, working every day in the shop.

Hope the world is treating you fine and please write again soon. Adios,
         Love, Bayer
p.s. Don, can you send those cigarettes now?

I CLOSED TOO MANY EYES

To: Mr. Donald Ross, (Sp) 2/c
Gunnery School
~~Naval Air Station~~
Seatle,
Washington

From: T/3 Bayer N. Ross
Med. Det. 3rd Bn.
16th Infantry
1st Inf. Div.
A P O 1,
New York City

Germany
June 15th, 1945

Dear Don & Lee_

  Have a few spare moments so thought I'd bat out a short V-Mail letter to you. Everything is going along fine over here at present and I haven't too much to do. Of course I realize that it can't last this way because in the past the army has always taken care of that and I-m sure they'll continue to do so in the future also.

  I still haven't heard anything about going home and it is beginning to look like it will be a little while yet before the ball starts to move around here. I don't mind too much though as long as I know I'll make it. I don't think I have to worry too much about the C.B.I. Surely wish I knew how Art stands on that score. The Army of Occupation is a pretty nice setup and I hope Art will be lucky enough to get a taste of it.

  You are probably back in Seatle now or at least on the way back. It must be hard to go back to work again after a leave to the old home town, isn't it?

  We've got shows in town now but I don't know whether I want to go or not. The place is generally too crowded for me.
  Hope you're well and happy and write soon.

T/3 Bayer Ross in his Hammelburg office, July 2, 1945

PART THREE:
After the War
(1945-1990)

Chapter 9

1945-1975

When Bayer got home on October 1, 1945 it didn't take him long to get back to work at the shop. Art was still in the Army stationed in Frankfurt and Don was still in the Navy as a gunnery instructor in Washington State. Don and Lee had been married in October 1944 and he wasn't discharged until December 1945. Bayer wasn't sure when either brother would be home but in the letters he wrote to Don over the month of October it was clear he needed Don's help with the dry cleaning business. **Here are three of those letters:**

Mountain Lake
October 8, 1945

Dear Don and Lee,
It's just a week since I arrived here. Boy! It's really wonderful to be back home again. Of course everything looked a bit different at first but I'm getting used to it. The biggest change was in Maxie. Gosh, I hardly recognized him. He must have gained a hundred pounds in the past three years.
Dad is terribly busy in the shop so I'm working a little trying to help him catch up some, but it's rather hard to do. That damn basket fills up with clothes as quick as you empty it.
Last night I went to St. James with some of the boys that are back home. I've never seen the place so quiet before. There just isn't anything going on anywhere.
Tubby Meyers got married Saturday to Irene Olson from Odin. I didn't expect that at least not so soon. He's been doing a lot of celebrating with Heppner and Foamy. Foamy left for Alabama to get his discharge. Johnny Janzen, the ex-sailor, was in the shop the other day. He's still the same Johnny except that he's married now too. His wife is a nurse stationed

at Great Lakes. He left Saturday to spend the weekend with her. I'm about the only single man left in town. I'll take that back – there's "Pinky" Klein too. I'm not bald headed yet so maybe there's still a chance.

I really feel out of place here. I miss my buddies I guess. Sort of hard to leave them after going through hell together for three years.

I took off my uniform just as soon as I got home. Boy, civilian clothes are hard to come by. Dad sold most of my clothes so I'm really hurting now. I'm going to have a hell of a time getting fixed up again but I suppose I'll manage.

I've been getting a lot of mail this past week coming back from Europe. I hadn't any when I was there for two months. Those pictures Lee sent were swell. Thanks a lot, Lee.

I think Art should be home by the first of the year. When are you going to get your discharge, Don? I wish you could come tomorrow. This place is dead without you. We were out to Judy's on Sunday. Boy are the kids ever big! Now I know I'm getting old.

It's past midnight so I better hit the hay. Take care of yourselves and write soon.

Love, Bayer

Mountain Lake
Sunday, October 14, 1945

Dear Don and Lee,
Hope all is well with you. We got our order finally for tuyeres for the stoker retort and Dad and I put them in this morning. The stoker works fine now. We are starting to get caught up a bit in the shop now. Dad says it hasn't been so empty in the back room since I left for the Army. So you see I haven't exactly been sitting around. I've been trying to get caught up completely so I could clean the place up a bit but everything takes so much time.

We had put in a new battery in the car the other day. I guess that makes three or four already for the old Ford. Something's wrong somewhere.

I CLOSED TOO MANY EYES

Bill Schroeder came back yesterday. The town is slowly getting back to normal. We've got a bowling alley in town now too. It's open weeknights only though. Even Bill Hayek opened up his pool hall the other day.

Remember that Armistice Day back in '41? Well, this is Armistice Day but not quite like that one. It was very cloudy and dark today – looks a bit like snow. Had to turn the lights on at 4 O'clock this afternoon. The snow we got the other day has just about disappeared now.

Uncle Carl and Anna are here from Rockford along with Gus. They've been here since Friday and plan to go back tomorrow but I don't know if they will or not.

Sarah is still working for us and once in a while we still have Mrs. Friesen too. Trying to get caught up completely if that's possible.

George Schraeder sold the theater to some lady from Mankato. I haven't seen a movie since I've been a civilian but one of these days I'll have to go.

I'm sending a bottle of perfume for Lee that I got in Paris. I've been wanting to do it ever since I got home but kept forgetting. I'm a poor authority on perfume so hope it's the right kind.

Lots of luck and hope to see you both soon.
            Love, Bayer

Mountain Lake
Monday, October 29, 1945

Dear Don and Lee,
Greetings from home! Today I went to work on the clarification tank. It took me all afternoon to get the dirt out of it and with a collection of tubs and pails I'm separating the alkali from about 30 gallons of solvent in the tank. Yesterday I took down the head of the ventilator over the press and reconnected the light. It's much better this way and gives more light in the room too.

I've said it to you before, but this town is Dead! Last night I took an excursion to St. James but there's nothing going on there either nor any other town around here. Quite a number of the boys are coming home now so that helps a bit.

Pinky Klein is putting on our storm windows, washing and puttying, etc. He's still the same old guy. Hunting season has been open for over a week now but the pheasants are really scarce. I didn't even bother to go out this year. I've got a pretty fair 20 gauge double barrel job that I picked up in Germany but haven't had time to clean it very well yet.

The other day I fixed the stoker a little. I took the motor off and mounted it outside the hopper with a larger belt and a larger pulley wheel on the motor. It turns the fan faster and works much better now. Of course a couple tuyeres are burned out but they've been on order for several months now so we'll just have to sweat them out.

I saw Harry Heppner last night. He's home on a furlough but for how long I don't know. I couldn't get much out of him since he was celebrating quite a bit.

I need a suit and overcoat but can't get any tailor-made so guess I'll have to get a stock job this time. If you can get me a few Arrow white shirts Don, I'll pay you double for them. These shirts here (if you rate high enough to get one) are almost like muslin.

A couple of Art's letters arrived this afternoon and he's still in Frankfurt. I think he'll get started to pull out very soon though.

I'd surely like to get out to Washington to see you both but I'd better not. Dad's been working too hard as it is and besides I really know what transportation is like now. I'd probably have to stand up on the bus or train the entire trip. And tires are plain too expensive yet.

Well, I better hit the hay. Please write soon.
             Love, Bayer

Don's journal entry describing coming home in December 1945 (typed by him in late 1990s)

I was discharged from the Navy on December 9, 1945. Coming home to Mt. Lake, from Seattle in our 1931 Ford, we stopped for gas. The garage man asked where we were headed. Minnesota. No, he said it's too much snow in the mountains and you don't even have chains on your tires. In those days, highways were not cleaned of snow as well as today. The 31 Ford has narrow tires and can go thru deep snow.

We were on our way home in the mountains and the car seemed to have very little power. I stopped to look at the engine. Looking at the rear of the car, I realized we had been climbing steadily for miles and didn't know it. I had to shift gears.

Later on the way home, somewhere in Idaho the car started to steam. I checked the oil and the dipstick said a foot of oil. It should have only 2 inches on the stick. What happened was that the head gasket leaked and all the water went into the oil pan! It probably was my fault, as I had put in some radiator cleaner and it must have been too strong and ate the gasket. We spent the nite in a hotel, while a garage overhauled it, and the next day we were on our way again.

Later on, on the way home the car had some trouble with the motor. Luckily, it happened right by a camp of "conscientious objectors". I was still in my Navy uniform. They refused to go into military service so the government allowed them to serve the country by doing voluntary service. Such as- hospital work, road repairs, forestry and other work. They did not believe in war and would not go. They had to prove they were religious and it was against their religion being taught. Otherwise, they would be put in prison for refusing to go into the Army. They were very good to us and fixed our car there.

We tried to save some money. Anti-freeze for the radiator was expensive. So, we drained the water out of the radiator every nite. Sometimes, the car wouldn't want to start in the morning after staying in a motel on the way home. We tried to park it the nite before on an incline so we would get it rolling, let out the clutch and then it started. About a year after we got home, we sold the 1931 Ford for $235.00. Made $20 dollars above original cost. Thought that was OK. Money was hard to get just then. Today, I could sell it for about $6000.00. Hind Sight!!

Being in the Navy for me was a fortunate expierence. I learned so much. I had wanted to serve overseas, but it never happened. Because of my education there, I was able to apply for the Postmaster position in Mt .Lake, which I held for 27 years.

1931 Ford

1945
Lois and Loren Halvorson
at his Graduation Dance at
Breck Academy

AUTHOR'S SUGGESTION:
Lois dated Loren Halvorson for a few years before he went off to St. Olaf College. He sadly passed away in 2010. See a couple online articles regarding The Reverend Dr. Halvorson: www.tinyurl.com/bayerross29 www.tinyurl.com/bayerross30

While Bayer and Don were reestablishing their team in the dry cleaning/tailoring shop in 1946, Bayer's future wife (my half-sister) Lois Kathleen Ruth Reno, graduated from Minneapolis's Marshall High School. That fall she started a two-year teaching certificate course at "Miss Woods' School" also in Minneapolis. Upon graduating from there in the summer of 1948, Lois took an offer from the elementary school in Mountain Lake to teach Kindergarten.

AUTHOR'S SUGGESTION:
See a website explaining the pioneering work in childhood education done by Miss Stella Wood:
www.tinyurl.com/bayerross28

Not long after beginning her teaching duties, Lois met Bayer when she brought some clothes in to be cleaned at Ross Cleaners. They dated for about a year and then announced they'd be married on June 18, 1950.

Bayer once told me he saw his life in two parts: not BEFORE and AFTER **the war**, but before and after **Lois**. In many ways things stayed the same in that he lived in the same town, did the same job, and had many of the same friends. He liked the familiarity of all that. That made him comfortable. He said he had always been a relaxed, laid back, small town fellow who admittedly was fanatical about satisfying his customers. He'd often stay at the shop until well after midnight finishing someone's suit and then deliver it at 7:00 am directly to the customer's house. He basically offered a free storage facility for the town's collective wardrobe because more often than not people would wait months before coming to get their dry cleaning – typically just before Easter, Thanksgiving or Christmas. That made for a poor revenue stream, but Bayer would never hound folks. It was like this from the day he returned from Europe until he and Lois moved to Minneapolis in the mid-1980s.

In the photo below, its Easter 1951 and the dinner is about to be served. On the far right is Lois's and my mother, Alma Arneson. My Dad, Clarence Arneson, is taking the photo. Lois had a different father, a Mr. Harry Reno, who unfortunately walked away from the family just months after Lois was born in 1928. I say "unfortunately," but I guess if that hadn't happened I wouldn't be standing there with that bow tie under my chin. Mother and Dad married in 1941 and I was born in 1946. That's Bayer and Lois on the far left, and you may notice that Lois is slightly "with child". Their **first** baby boy, **David Lynn Ross**, was born on May 24th. Their **second** son, **Jon Paul Ross** was born May 5, 1954, and son **number 3, Steven James Ross** came along on July 30, 1957. Next to Lois and Bayer in the photo are mother's sister Thelma, her husband Frank Nelson, and their son Vernon Ross Nelson. Finally. Between Alma and Thelma are their parents, my grandparents, Rasmus and Carrie Thorson.

And in the next photo, Jon (at left) is six, David is nine, and Steve is soon to turn three. It's 1960, and in a few weeks we'd all be celebrating at the annual Mountain Lake "Pow Wow." For a few days in June the town basically throws a party with a Pow Wow parade and a square-block park filled with carnival rides, concession stands, and for years an open-pit full-steer barbeque where everyone at no charge got two slices of bread and a generous portion of beef. At the end of Pow Wow the city fathers would pull the name of the lucky winner of a new car generously provided to the city at cost by a local car dealer. Bayer was an active member of Mountain Lake's American Legion Post and he and Don would march every year in the parade in full Legion uniform. Bayer would also work at the Legion's Pow Wow hamburger stand flipping burgers.

**Home of Bayer and Lois Ross
Mountain Lake, Minnesota**

Bayer only had a few blocks to walk from their house to the shop. And the boys only had a few blocks to walk to school. In fact, everyone had only a few blocks to walk to anywhere in

Mountain Lake. The house had a cistern system to collect rain water on the roof and deliver it down to a storage tank in the basement. Very 19th Century! Great source of free water for cleaning and laundry. There was a large living room, dining room, eat-in kitchen, half bath, and a study on the first floor and four bedrooms and full bath on the second floor. The upstairs toilet was called "The Throne" because of its elevation off the floor similar to the one in this photo. Why was it elevated? No one knew.

There from left to right in the photo above is Jon, David (holding our son, Craig) and Steven in 1973. They all turned out to be pillars in their communities. All three of Lois and Bayer's boys have embraced music as an important part of their lives. Jon plays and teaches piano and writes music, David plays several instruments and has been in a band for years, and Steven is an accomplished guitarist and a DJ on a local radio station. Our son, Craig, loves almost every musical genre and has an MP3 collection probably as large the one owned by the Rock and Roll Hall of Fame.

This photo was taken on Bayer's 56th birthday in 1973. All four of the Ross sibling... Max, Don, Judy, and Bayer...together. Sadly, their parents, John and Lillie had passed away by then.

Chapter 10

1976-1990

Betty, Craig and I were living in Fairborn, Ohio in 1977 when Bayer, Lois and my folks came for a visit. I was getting a Master's Degree at the time at the Air Force Institute of Technology at Wright Paterson Air Force Base. So here is Bayer, Lois and Craig with my mother peeking around the corner.

I CLOSED TOO MANY EYES

On June 5, 1986, after I graduated from another year-long Air Force program, this time at the National Defense University in Washington DC, Betty, Craig, and I flew into Rhein Main Air Base near Frankfurt, Germany on an Air Force C-5 cargo plane.

We spent a couple weeks on our own in England and Wales and then went back to Frankfurt to await the arrival of Lois and Bayer. They arrived on June 22nd and together we first went all over Germany so Bayer could revisit some places he'd seen during the war. Then in July we spent about three weeks touring Denmark, Sweden, and Norway. In Malmo, Sweden we visited Bayer's second cousin Willy Pearson and his wife Barbro and then went to Bayer's cousin Margit's home and her brother, Ernst, joined us. A few days later we were in Hudiksvall, Sweden visiting Bayer's Uncle John Jonasson and his wife Signe. In Norway we got to see relatives of Lois and my maternal grandmother and grandfather. Bayer and Lois flew back to the States from Frankfurt on Friday, July 18th.

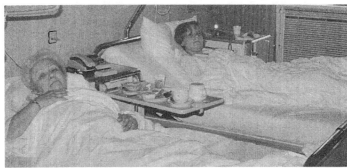

Lois spent the first night in Europe in a German hospital (fatigue)

Bayer, close to the spot he and the 16th Infantry Regiment crossed the Rhine River in 1945 (41 years earlier)

Bayer and Craig in the Bavarian countryside

The year after we returned from our Grand Tour, Lois and Bayer sold their house in Mountain Lake and moved to Minneapolis. It was 1987 and Bayer had turned 70 and Lois, 59. Bayer passed away from a heart attack in 1990 as he was walking to his car in the Apache Plaza shopping center parking lot. He was leaving the Waldorf Cleaners where he was working part time. Lois passed away after a bad fall in 2013.

PART FOUR:
Family Scrapbook

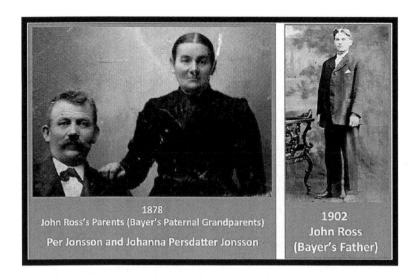

1878
John Ross's Parents (Bayer's Paternal Grandparents)
Per Jonsson and Johanna Persdatter Jonsson

1902
John Ross
(Bayer's Father)

Bayer's paternal grandparents, **Per** (1858-1936) and **Johanna** (1855-1922) **Jonsson**

They had eight children (all born in Malmo, Sweden)

- (1) Bengta (also called Betty, Bessie) Carlson 1879-1955 Married John Carlson (Lived in Minnesota)
- (2) Maria (Mary) Hoffman 1881-1956 (Lived in Minnesota) Married John Hoffman
- (3) Andrew Johnson 1882-1947 (Lived in Colorado)
- (4) **John Ross 1885-1964 (Bayer's Father)**
- (5) August (Gus) Johnson 1887-1964 (Lived in Colorado, Minnesota, and Illinois)
- (6) Henning Jonsson 1888-1911 (Lived in Sweden)
- (7) Wilhelm Persson (derived from father's name) 1891-1966
  (Lived in Sweden) Married Ingeborg and had two children, Marget and Ernst
- (8) Anna Persson 1894-1951 (Lived in Sweden) Married Karl Persson and had four children, Marta, Yegve, Ruth and Per

AUTHOR'S SUGGESTION:
See a 5-minute video on Malmo, Sweden where Bayer's father was from: www.tinyurl.com/bayerross31

Bayer's maternal grandparents, Anders (1856-1931) and **Anna** (1864-1946) **Jonasson**

PAUL S. ARNESON

They had 10 children (all born in Hudiksvall, Sweden)

(1) Hannah Matilda Johnson 1886-1970
Married Andrew and later his brother August (Lived in Colorado, Minnesota and Illinois)
(2) Karl Reinhold Jonasson 1890-1965 (Lived in Sweden)
(3) **Lillie Charlotte Jonasson Ross 1892-1955 (Bayer's Mother)**
(4) Einar Johnson 1894-1976 (Lived in Illinois)
Married Agnes Welander Johnson
(5) Maja (Marie) Jonasson Carlson 1896-1966 (Lived in Illinois) Married to Gus Carlson
(6) Gertrude Linnea Jonasson Tornquist 1898-1988 (Lived in Illinois) Married to Vilhelm (William, Bill) Tornquist
(7) Oskar (Oscar) Nils Jonasson 1899-1962 (Lived in Illinois)
(8) Fred (Fritz) Anders Johnson 1901-1952 (Lived in Illinois)
(9) Berger (Ben) Johnson 1906-1958 (Lived in Illinois)
(10) John Edvin Jonasson 1908-1994 (Lived in Sweden) Married to Signe Jonasson

1931 The Jonassons
Fritz Einar Gertrude Ben Oscar
Hannah Maja Anna Lilly

The photo above harbors a sad story. It was taken just a few days after Bayer's Grandfather, Anders Jonasson, had died. Anders and Anna had been in the U.S. visiting their children when he came down with what they thought was the flu. They were to return to Hudiksvall, Sweden in another week but he succumbed to pneumonia. Instead of returning the body to Sweden, he was buried in Chicago. The photo above shows all the children but Karl and John who never immigrated to America. All eight others had. Anna returned to Sweden not long after Ander's funeral. She sadly died after being hit by a car in 1946.

AUTHOR'S SUGGESTION:
See a 4-minute video on Hudiksvall, Sweden where Bayer's mother was from: www.tinyurl.com/bayerross32. Be sure to see it in FULL SCREEN mode. Absolutely beautiful!

1915
John and Lillie
Genoa, CO

Two months after arriving in America and Lillie is still smiling above. The story goes that both of them had visions of leading a cowboy/cowgirl sort of life once they settled "out west". In the photo he even has a cowboy hat in hand and she's got a (somewhat) western outfit on too. But the rattlesnakes, the drought, the heat, and the loneliness sent them packing and heading to Minnesota.

1915 Three Brothers Homesteading Genoa, Colorado
John, Andrew, and August (Gus)

AUTHOR'S SUGGESTION:
See a 5-minute video on Genoa, Colorado's history as told through the *somewhat* famous "Genoa Tower" built in the 1920s: www.tinyurl.com/bayerross33

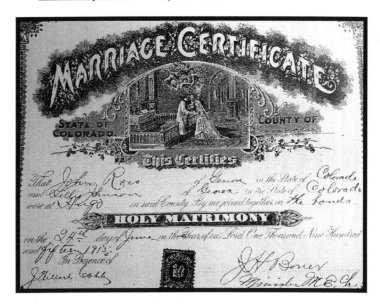

AUTHOR'S SUGGESTION:
See a 48-minute video recording (made in 2014) of Don Ross reminiscing about the "good old days". It's Bayer's son, Jon, heard off-camera: www.tinyurl.com/bayerross38

AUTHOR'S SUGGESTION:
See a 7-minute video of Mountain Lake taken from a drone launched by a town resident in 2016. The quality is absolutely amazing: www.tinyurl.com/bayerross35

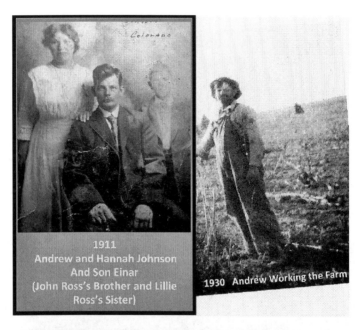

1911 Andrew and Hannah Johnson And Son Einar (John Ross's Brother and Lillie Ross's Sister)

1930 Andrew Working the Farm

1925 John Ross and Chickens Windom, MN

John Ross, who for fourteen years has been associated with John Hoffman in the tailoring business in Windom, has leased rooms in the David Ewert building, and will open a cleaning and tailoring shop next week. Mr. Ross expects to install a dry cleaning plant within a short time. Sept 1, 1927

Mountain Lake OBSERVER Newspaper

1939 Dry Cleaning Plant Behind Shop

1928 Don Ross

1931
Anna and Anders Jonasson
And daughter Gertrude

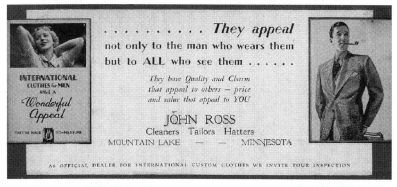

1924
Wilhelm & Ingeborg
Jonsson
Ernst and Margit

1956
Wilhelm & Ingeborg
Jonsson

Mr. and Mrs. August (Gus) Johnson
Hannah and Gus
(Lillie Ross's Sister and John Ross's Brother)

1949
Hannah Married Gus After
Andrew Passed Away

PAUL S. ARNESON

ARTHUR M. ROSS, son of Mr. and Mrs. John Ross, is another of Mountain Lake's servicemen who saw most of the European theatre of war. Art came home Monday with his discharge from the U. S. Army. He has been in the army almost four years has been overseas since the middle of 1943.

Arthur Ross

Arthur Ross, 82, of Berwyn, Ill., died Dec. 12, 1998.

Services were held Dec. 15, at North Riverside, Ill., with Rev. Joel Chrastka officiating.

Arthur Mark Ross was born to John and Lilly Jonasson Ross in Windom March 6, 1916. The family moved to Mt. Lake in 1927. His parents started a Tailor and Dry Cleaning business, later named Ross Cleaners.

Arthur attended the public school in Mt. Lake. He then worked for George P. Neufeld Variety Store, where he also roasted sunflower seeds, packaged them and delivered them to the neighboring communities for resale.

He served in the U.S. Army during World War II. His duties included guarding the locks at Sault Ste. Marie, Mich. Returning after the war, Aruthur worked for a time at Ross Cleaners.

He married Helen Johnson from Jackson. They attended Bethel Church where he was also an usher. They later moved to Chicago to serve a term doing missionary work in the Woodlawn area.

He later married Ethel Gaa, whom he met at West Suburban Hospital where he worked for 20 years.

He was preceded in death by his sister, Judith College, and two brothers, Max and Bayer.

Survivors include four stepdaughters and their families in Chicago and one brother, Donald (Lee) Ross and family of Mt. Lake.

I CLOSED TOO MANY EYES

Max Bayer Art Don Lillie John

1952 The John Ross Family (daughter Judy missing)

PAUL S. ARNESON

HISTORY OF THE DRY CLEANING AND TAILORING BUSINESS IN MOUNTAIN LAKE, MINNESOTA

As recorded by John Ross in 1947:

John Franz, father of Mrs. J.J. Balzer, was a tailor by trade in Russia. Mrs. Balzer was the mother of Dr. Harvey Balzer. When he came to America in the late 1800s, John Franz went into farming, while his daughter, Mrs. J.J. Balzer, eventually picked up needle and thread. In the early days she sewed and altered clothing and made shrouds or burial garments, mainly for women and children. In later life she had a shop in the "Annex" or hotel where she sewed, mended, and altered clothing for both men and women. Philip Nerstheimer from Austria, operated a tailor shop in Mountain Lake for some years before we established the Ross Shop in 1927. Our first shop was east and north of the David Ewert Glass Block store (corner of 3rd Avenue and 9th Street)

AUTHOR'S SUGGESTION:
Visit a webpage giving a history of Mountain Lake written by resident John Jungas (circa around 1970):
www.tinyurl.com/bayerross36

AUTHOR'S SUGGESTION:
A truly fascinating free 627-page e-book written in 1916 detailing the early history of Cottonwood and Watonwan Counties in Minnesota. If you are a Mountain Lake history buff (or want to be), you need to see this:
www.tinyurl.com/bayerross37

I CLOSED TOO MANY EYES

An excerpt:

STRUGGLES OF PIONEER SETTLERS.

The early settlers of this county had anything but a promising outlook. Prairie fires and terrible hail storms swept away much of the property of the settlers in their destructive pathways, but these hardy sons and daughters felt determined to fight their way through these obstacles and adversities. The crop of 1872 was an average crop and the people felt encouraged. In the spring of 1873 a large crop was planted, and the immigrants of previous years, not only of this but of adjoining counties, had expended every resource in preparing the ground and providing seed. A promising harvest was apparent; and all felt that the reward for their severe privations would soon be at hand. But alas, early in June of that year the entire part of southwestern Minnesota was visited by grasshoppers, and nearly all of the growing crops were destroyed and grasshopper eggs laid and buried in the soil, only to curse the country the next season. Great desolation was among the farmers. Appeals made to the charitable throughout the better favored sections of the country brought considerable immediate relief. In the Legislature in January, 1874, an appropriation of five thousand dollars was made for relief of the devastated regions and, later, twenty-five thousand dollars was appropriated for the purchase of seed grain.

Judith College

MOUNTAIN LAKE — Services for Judith College, 6?, Mountain Lake, who died Tuesday at Mountain Lake Community Hospital, will be 2 p.m. Saturday at Alliance Missionary Church, Mountain Lake. Burial will be in Mountain Lake Cemetery.

Visitation will be 2 to 9 p.m. Friday at Eifert Funeral Home, Mountain Lake, and 9 a.m. until services at the church.

Born May 9, 1920, in Windom, she moved with her parents to Mountain Lake in 1927. She married Edwin L. College on July 4, 1939, in Northwood, Iowa. They lived on a farm east of Mountain Lake until 1973 when they moved into Mountain Lake. She was active in Alliance Missionary Church.

She is survived by her husband, Edwin; three daughters, Betty (Mrs. Leo) Steiner, North St. Paul, Shirley (Mrs. John) Michaels, Mountain Lake, and Sandra (Mrs. Tom) Hanson, Butterfield; two sons, Eldon, St. Paul, and Eugene, Omaha, Neb.; four brothers, Bayer and Donald Ross, both of Mountain Lake, Max Ross, Minneapolis, and Arthur Ross, Chicago, Ill.; and 8 grandchildren.

The Ed College Family

Bayer's sister Judith passed away in 1981. Her husband, Ed, was an insurance salesman after farming for several years. The College's were known for their excellent livestock and often won prizes at the Minnesota State Fair for their hogs and cattle.

PAUL S. ARNESON

All Advertisements from the **Mountain Lake OBSERVER**:

The 4th War Loan Starts Jan. 18

Maybe you won't be glad to see him home after all!

ONE DAY, your man will come home. Home—after having done his duty and played his part in the bitterest, cruelest fight of all time.

And you?

Will you be able to welcome him back with nothing but sheer joy and thankfulness in your heart?

Or will the sight of him remind you, for the rest of your life, that even though your job was unutterably easier than his, you still didn't do it —you didn't quite measure up?

That would be a miserable thing to have happen to you. It would be a miserable feeling to carry through the years.

So don't take any chances. Don't just buy your share of War Bonds. Do that—and then do more. And do it today.

There are Bonds for Every Type of Investor----The Best Securities Available.
It's our privilege as well as our duty to BUY MORE BONDS

This Advertisement Sponsored by the Following Patriotic Mountain Lake Firms and Individuals

REMPEL'S BARBER SHOP	MOUNTAIN LAKE IMPLEMENT CO.
MOUNTAIN LAKE CO-OP. CREAMERY	H. J. NIESSEN, Standard Oil Agent
PERSONALITY BEAUTY SHOPPE	CO-OPERATIVE FARMERS ELEVATOR
LA DONNA'S BEAUTY SALON	SWIFT & COMPANY
DR. R. L. WENBERG, D. D. S.	HUBBARD & PALMER
ROSS CLEANERS	NORTH STAR TELEPHONE CO.
DR. EDW. WIDDELL, Optometrist	WORTHINGTON CREAMERY & PRODUCE

Mountain Lake .... War Production Center!

Except for the growing number of stars in service flags, few outward signs reveal that we in this community are engaged in the grimmest sort of war.

Yet our community—and particularly this farmer co-operative—are gearing nearly all our daily efforts to meeting the needs of war.

This co-operative today is a WAR INDUSTRY— equally as much as any steel mill, shipyard or airplane factory in America!

Our job is part of the greatest mass production job in history — securing the tremendous amounts of food America needs for our armed forces, our allies, our home front and the starving nations of the world!

This cooperative is doing its full share!

In doing the job we recognize all the implications of our responsibility. We believe that America must have all the dairy products it will be possible to produce. We also believe that this cooperative's reputation for producing quality dairy products must be maintained both during the war and in the years of peace to come. So, today, as always, our members and our employees are devoted to producing dairy products of highest quality.

This is our solemn pledge:

WE SHALL CONTINUE TO PRODUCE THE FOOD AMERICA NEEDS ... MAINTAINING HIGHEST QUALITY ... UNTIL VICTORY AND BEYOND!

MOUNTAIN LAKE CO-OP. CREAMERY

J. M. FRANZ, President   A. H. EWERT, Vice President   D. H. SCHROEDER, Sec'y
JOHN D. QUIRING, W. J. BEHRENDS, H. T. NICKEL, JAC. F. LOEWEN, Directors
WALTER RUCKER, Manager

A MEMBER COOPERATIVE OF LAND O'LAKES CREAMERIES, INC.

HOME FRONT WAR CRY!

Plant a VEGETABLE VICTORY GARDEN

JUST THINK!—one-fifth of our total food production for 1943 must go to meet the needs of our armed forces and allies! This includes one-half of our commercial canned goods! The answer is VICTORY GARDENS! Buy complete supplies from JUNGAS now!

Check This Supply List:

RAKES	FORKS	SPADES
HOES	TROWELS	GLOVES
SEEDS	SHEARS	INSECTICIDES

FRESH VEGETABLE SEEDS

6 pkgs. for **25c**

VIGORO VICTORY FERTILIZER
5 Lbs. 50c
10 Lbs. 80c
25 Lbs. $1.40

Milorganite
6c Lb.
25 Lbs. $1.25

Jungas Hardware Co.

Telephone 98   Mountain Lake

PAUL S. ARNESON

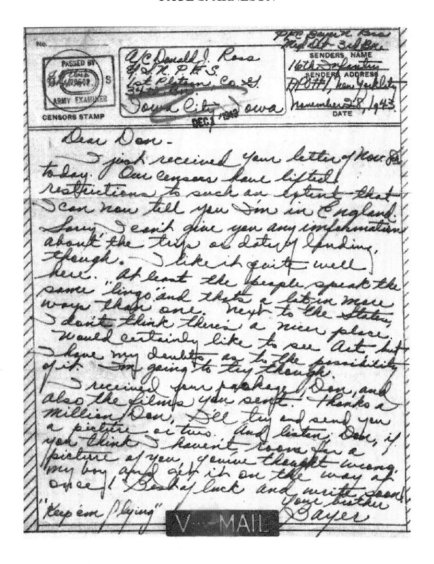

HAVEMEIER-ROSS 1944

Miss Leola Havemeier and Donald Ross S 2|c, were married Saturday evening, October 21 in Seattle, Washington. The ceremony was performed in St. Paul's Lutheran church. A wedding dinner was served in a Seattle hotel, following the ceremony.

Mrs. Ross was employed in the Dr. P. J. Pankratz office in Mountain Lake before the doctor left for military service. Seamen second class Ross has been in the navy since April, 1943, and recently has been instructing flying officers in aerial gunnery.

He is a son of Mr. and Mrs. John Ross of Mountain Lake, and Mrs. Ross' parents live near Courtland.

1954
John and Lillie Ross
Lee Ross with son Rob and daughter Jane

1995 Alma Arneson (Lois's and Author's Mother) and Jane Ross

1928 John and Signe Jonasson

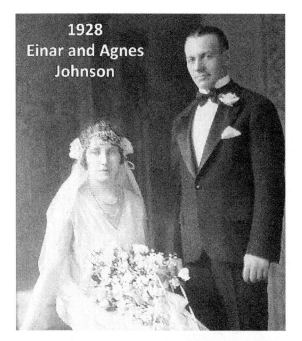

1928 Einar and Agnes Johnson

1940 Mother Anna with John & Signe Jonasson

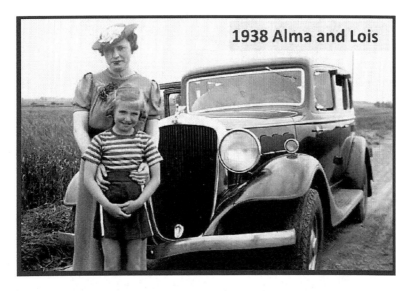

**1948
Lois and Paul**

AUTHOR'S NOTE:
Lois turned 18 the year I was born (1946). She graduated from Marshall High School in Minneapolis that year.

1949 - Lois

1953
Carrie Thorson (Lois's and Author's Maternal Grandmother) and Lillie Ross

1955 Lillie Ross

I CLOSED TOO MANY EYES

Lilly Charlotte Ross

Lilly Charlotte Ross, daughter of Mr. and Mrs. Andrew Jonsson, was born at Hudiksvall, Sweden on March 20, 1892. In 1913 she came to America where she settled near Genoa, Colorado. On June 24, 1915, she was united in marriage to John Ross at Hugo, Colorado. The couple established a home in Windom. Five children came to bless their home. In 1927 they moved to Mountain Lake, where they have since made their home.

Mother was in apparently good health, never one to complain, she was up and about her household duties. On Monday afternoon at 4:45 p. m., November 21, 1955, she was taken suddenly to be with her Heavenly Father. At the day of her passing she was 63 years, 8 months and 1 day old.

Mrs. Ross was a kind and loving wife, mother and grandmother, always doing something for somebody else.

She is survived by her husband, one daughter, Judith, Mrs. Edwin College of Mt. Lake; four sons, Arthur, Bayer, Donald, all of Mt. Lake, and Max of Minneapolis. Also surviving are three daughters-in-law, one son-in-law, and ten grandchildren; three sisters, Hannah of Rockford, Ill.; Gertrude and Marie of Chicago, Ill.; five brothers, Ben, Oscar and Einar, all of Chicago, Ill., and John and Karl, who live in Sweden. Also a host of friends and other relatives.

Mother is and will be sadly missed by all. May God bless her precious memory.

—The Family

John Ross, Mt. Lake Businessman, Dies

John Ross, Mt. Lake businessman since 1927, passed away at Bethel hospital Monday evening, Jan. 20 at the age of 79. Mr. Ross had been ailing since October, 1963. Death was due to cancer.

He came to Mt. Lake in 1927 and established the Ross Cleaners and Tailors.

A pleasant, congenial businessman, Mr. Ross dedicated his time to the tailoring and dry cleaning business. His sons inherited this interest and two of them, Bayer and Donald, remained in Mt. Lake to work with him.

Survivors include five children: Arthur, Chicago, Ill.; Bayer and Don, Mt. Lake; Max, Minneapolis; and Judith, Mrs. Edwin College, Mt. Lake; 12 grandchildren; two brothers: Wilhelm Johnson in Sweden, and August Johnson, Rockford, Ill. His wife preceded him in death in 1955.

Funeral services will be held on Friday, Jan. 24, 1:30 p.m., at Johnson Chapel and 2 p.m. at the Alliance Missionary church. The Rev. Irvin Malm will officiate at the services. Burial will be in the Mt. Lake cemetery.

PAUL S. ARNESON

1950

Made in the USA
Lexington, KY
28 May 2018